AF423357

ORIENT F.C.

A PICTORIAL HISTORY

By Neil Kaufman & Alan Ravenhill

London
Jupiter Books

The publishers would like to offer their thanks for the assistance given them by Mr. Douglas Tilley, Orient's official photographer, many of whose photos have been used. We would also like to thank the two local newspapers who have supplied us with help and photos, *The Walthamstow Guardian* and *The Stratford Express*.

JUPITER BOOKS (LONDON) LTD
167 Hermitage Road, London, N.4

Printed and bound in Great Britain
by Tinling (1973) Ltd, Prescot, Merseyside

Contents

Foreword

ORIENT FOOTBALL CLUB

From the smallest to the largest, or the thinnest to the thickest of encyclopaedias or dictionaries, one will inevitably find a multitude of explanations concerning the word "Orient".

The Far East; Asia; the value of a pearl; its brilliance; its originality; adjustment to a situation; a form of culture and I have even read that it refers to the "establishment of a relationship with others by placing or arranging in a certain manner".

Irrespective of whatever the experts may say, there are four or five thousand regular supporters of the Orient Football Club to whom the word means so much more.

When one examines the ninety-two club names in the English Football League, there are only two without a geographical tag, ourselves and our near neighbours and competitors, the Arsenal. How much more difficult must it be to create support, allegiance and following, when one does not have a titled catchment area, in which young people growing up support a football team because its name relates to the area in which they live, such as Tottenham, West Ham, Chelsea, Fulham, etc.

We, at the Orient, so we read, have been cinderellas, poor relations, underdogs as well as many other descriptions, both complimentary and otherwise.

Those of us that have supported the club over the years, however, know that there now exists, within every section and level of support, a spirit and determination to succeed, the like of which has not been matched in the past, either by our own club or any other.

I have the privilege of being Chairman of a Board of Directors whose enthusiasm and drive must inevitably contribute to success. I have the pleasure of working with George Petchey whose ability is beyond doubt, and his team of helpers and advisers, whose loyalty and expertise, must also contribute a great deal to the cause.

What of the players? Well, for me to comment on their ability would be unfair and ill-advised as I neither have the intricate knowledge of football or the experience to do so, but what I can evaluate is their loyalty, determination and team spirit, all of which are beyond doubt and, once again, must be the ingredients to success.

Any gastronomical delight or specialised pudding lacking of an ingredient, let alone the most important one, will not give satisfaction or prove successful. Therefore, to leave out the most vital ingredient in our plan of success for the future, would be wrong, and I refer, of course, to our supporters. Old and young, six foot fours and four foot elevens, male and female, venturing forth in all weathers, returning home elated or depressed, they continue with the same spirit of support, and will to do better things. I can sum up my respect and admiration for them by referring to them as people you can count on.

Really all the people, be they players, management, office staff, Directors, groundsmen are, at the Orient, people you can count on.

The glamour of the big clubs, whilst attractive, has its own built-in self-destruction, but the sincerity of the Orient will bring inevitable success and ensure continued spirit; and will always attract the kind of supporter that we will all be happy to stand or sit beside at any match.

In the book that follows, I am sure there will be created for the older supporter a great deal of nostalgia and for the younger supporter confirmation of some of the stories heard on the terraces and an introduction to some of the past that has, as yet, not reached their ears. Mostly I believe that it will, for all those reading, make more understandable the creation of the springboard on which we now stand, ready poised to do better things.

Those of you reading about the Orient, although not supporters, will, I hope, be encouraged into paying us a visit; for having once stood on our terraces or having sat in our stands, you will be attracted to return.

I am sure that all of us can be proud not only of a fine beginning and history, but can be certain that we will all be proud of the future that is just around the corner. This is my opportunity of thanking everybody and saying I recognize you are all people that I can count on.

Brian Winston

Early Days

The early days of the Clapton Orient Football Club are incompletely recorded, but certain facts are known. Some members of the Clapton Park Cricket Club committee, who worked for Orient Shipping, got together with a group of the company's clerks and in the summer of 1881 the club was born. The name Clapton Park Football Club was naturally suggested, but the general feeling was for something new, and the name Clapton Orient was chosen.

By September the first organised matches were being played in competitions in and around Clapton. They remained an amateur club for over twenty years, and in 1888 when the Football League was formed the club was still very small. Around 1890 the team, now playing in the Metropolitan Amateur League, wore red shirts with a big letter O on their backs in white (there were no shirt numbers then) and white shorts. This is believed to be the time the shouts of 'up the O's' first really stuck. From about 1891-4 the Orient played in the South Eastern League and in the Great Western League, and in 1896 they were the founder members of the London League. They finished runners-up in this league and as the team improved support began to grow.

Their first home was a primitive ground next to the Clapton Cricket Club. They moved, first to Clapton rugby and cricket grounds (and it was from 1892-6 that they also played at the Pond Lane Bridge ground), where they used Great Eastern Railroad coaches for dressing rooms. The entrance fee was 3d and if by any chance supporters were bored by the football, they could always look over the fence and watch the whippet racing next door. In the event the club was forced to move by the borough council, who wanted the ground for an electric power station. It was at the whippet ground that the club moved into professional ranks even though most of the O's players were still amateurs and the reserve team were unpaid. In the latter part of 1901 the team played its first professional match, not in the League but a friendly, winning 12-0. In 1902, now down the Millfields Road at Bailey's Firework ground, it was decided to build a proper stadium and, by using the slag from the power station, terracing soon began to rise. In 1902/3 the reserves were runners-up in the Metropolitan League, level with Leytonstone FC, and during this season the O's won the Middlesex Senior Cup. They were outgrowing the London League and applied for Southern League membership in 1903, but were rejected. They were turned down again the following season, and this determined them to make an all-out bid for the Football League, though without too much hope in their chances.

The team changed its colours to red, white and green striped shirts with white shorts. In 04/5 the vote went against them for election to the Football League. However, the League's management at this time wanted to extend the number of clubs, and so Orient finally made it, along with Chelsea, Hull City, Leeds United and Stockport County into Division 2. More directors were then invited to join the board: Mr. Ludford, a glass bottling merchant from Brooksby Road, and a Mr. F. Snewin, a dairyman of Upper Clapton who later became mayor of

Hackney.

Looking back again to the club's amateur days, Orient had a notable centre-forward in 1890 called Harry Edgar. He was tall, had a big moustache and was perhaps a bit crude when it came to the skills of the game. He would hang around the halfway mark when Orient were defending but when he got the ball he would punt it forward and gallop after it in his ungainly style. But he often scored. He had a way with the officials too, and once argued them into awarding his colleague, Freddy Nesbit, a goal in a local cup-tie when there was doubt whether his shot went under or over the cross-rope (there were no posts then).

The Millfields Road ground was improved and it was thought they could pack in about 12,000. During 1905 they applied to join the Southern League division 1. The club was to be converted into a limited company and the ground would be reconstructed to hold a capacity of 40,000. The manager was to be Sam Ormerod from Manchester City. It must be remembered that many of the players, managers and trainers of the 1881-1905 period, though not known by name were the pioneers who dug a path for the Orient of later years. Such players, apart from H. Edgar (1890-?) and F. Nesbit (1890-1), as J. Wright (92-5), G. Smith (1900-3), J. Shorter (1899-1902), and also H. Kingaby, W. Codling, P. Proudfoot and J. Boden, who stayed with the O's through the early years in the Football League. These were the only players retained from the non-League days by the new manager, Sam Ormerod. Money was now needed to recruit and mould his new team, and for the ground improvements being made. Financial problems made this a shaky start to the League campaign, and the players were obliged to change in horse-drawn tramcars and pass through the crowd to reach the pitch.

The very first game in the League was on 2nd September 1905 away at Leicester Fosse. Kingaby scored Orient's first goal.

In the last few seconds of the match Morgan scored from 30 yards to clinch it 2-1 for Leicester. They also lost the first home game, on 9th September, 1-0 to Hull City; 3,000 saw Kingaby's late goal ruled offside. On the following Monday afternoon they beat Glossop 2-0—first blood. But they were unsteady on their feet, gaining only six points from the first ten games, and in fact they managed only seven wins in the whole season.

In the FA cup Orient drew 1-1 against and then beat Falstead 5-1. They then beat Barking 3-1, and Clapton 2-0 in front of 4,000 home fans, but lost 3-0 the replay with Chesterfield having held them 0-0 at home. They were bottom of the League at end of the season. Not an inspiring start, though the players (on a maximum wage of £4 per week) were seldom outclassed.

FIRST SEASON—FIRST MONEY CRISIS

By November the team were a dangerous third from bottom. By January (1906) there was talk of a financial crisis, rumours were flying, some pleasant, some not. An investigation revealed that some influential shareholders had taken over the club. It got around that Bert Kingaby was to be transferred to Arsenal, and supporters put this advert in the local paper:

Please Mr. Kingaby stay with us do
Your wing work is A1 tricky and true
If you, greatest of runners
Did go to the gunners
You would leave the poor old O's in a stew.

Kingaby decided to stay on. And the club had friends. A large building firm offered to complete the grandstand. Captain Wells-Holland, the former mayor of Hackney offered to become a director and the famous Alan Haigh-Brown came to play for us. Then a creditor filed a petition for the compulsory winding-up of the company. £200-£300 was needed immediately if the reconstruction scheme was to be saved, and a shareholder had to give £50 just to ensure the remaining fixtures could be honoured. The team showed no signs of worry, going out in front of 5,000 at Millfields Road to thrash Burnley 3-0, Kingaby putting in two.

A newspaper said: "The position of the club is a mystery. With such districts as Hackney and Homerton to draw from, one would have thought that the financial success of the team was assured." Ex-O's captain, R. P. Haines saw that 'it would be nothing less than calamity for local sport if one of the oldest and most progressive clubs in London comes to an end.' A strong committee under Wells-Holland was elected and their appeal for support met with ready response, though Kingaby and Boden had to go to Aston Villa in the end. A plan was then put forward for a new company, Clapton Orient Football Club Ltd., with £3,000 capital to be divided into 1,200 shares at 5/- each to be credited with 3s 9d paid.

It was obvious to manager Ormerod that some members of the side had to be replaced. Orient only gained re-election to division 2 by a single vote over Oldham Athletic, then new applicants. (We have never had to apply again). The following season 06/7 was much better although the fans would have liked the improvement to be faster. They finished fourth from bottom in the table, and fielded a reserve team in the Southern League. All in all they did well considering the pressure on the players —another season in bottom position and that would have been goodbye to League soccer.

With experience the team was improving, and more people were prepared to support them and Sam Ormerod. They barely scraped the first 07/8 game, beating Hull 1-0, then three days later gained a 2-2 draw at Barnsley. Injuries led to Blackpool taking revenge for last season's defeat, beating the weakened team 5-0. Again their away record let them down, 12 goals against 52 hit past them. Over all they scored 40 goals and finished in 14th position. They went to the third round of the Cup, going out to Southend 3-1 in a replay down on the coast.

Then Billy Holmes took over from Sam Ormerod, the team's guide through the earliest years. Under Holmes they went through a cruel start to the 08/9 season and in all it was not a very successful term; they scored only 37 goals from 38 matches ending fifteenth. There was a crying need for a forceful goalscorer. Parker, Candy and Prior all showed ability; Louch could have been the man, but was an amateur and wasn't always available. In the Cup we went down 5-0 to top of Division One Newcastle United, in a snow-storm. But the spirit of the team showed on and off the football field. Wells-Holland, the O's director, set up a fund for the Wigan colliery disaster, and many hospitals and nurses homes benefitted by Orient's actions.

Parker opened the 09/10 season with both goals against Loughborough Trinity, a header and a splendid 20 yarder. At home the team wore their new colours, white shirts with red V's and black shorts and very nice they looked as well. 20,000 saw visiting Manchester City go down 3-2 again Parker scored two. The little winger Underwood had a great game and scored the third. In the last week of the season Fred Parker became the first to make 100 League appearances for Orient. The team finished 16th, and went down to West Bromwich 2-0 in the Cup. At this time many people in the provinces called Orient 'The Homerton Chinamen' or 'The Orientals of Homerton'.

The sixth season 10/1 was the best so far, and they made a great start. Bevan, Scott, Goffin and Parker were the strikers when they won 3-0 at Stockport on 3rd September, 1-0 over a strong Derby side, and 3-0 at Leicester Fosse: 8 points from 4 matches. One northern manager summed up Orient thus: 'They may not be the most brilliant side around but they always help one another so well and they never say die until the final whistle.' Many people nicknamed the O's 'Holmes' Homerton Heroes'.

In the Cup the Gunners won the return 2-1. But the run-in produced good enough results to ensure them the 4th position.

In consequence the 11/2 season was even more exciting for the fans, now eager for promotion to the big League. 13,846 poured into the home ground to see Derby go down 3-0 to the shooting power of Dix, Scott and, signing of the season, McFadden from Wallsend Park FC. In January they lost in front of 45,000 at Chelsea. G. Johnson, the curly haired back was transferred to Chelsea soon after, so ending the 'J.J.' defence partnership. In the Cup, they kept Everton's famous goalie Scott busy, but lost 2-1. In the evening the match was run on the bioscope at the Clapton cinematograph theatre. 11,000 saw the real thing, paying £556 in receipts, and thousands more flocked to see it on the screen. Later on they won the London Challenge Cup for the first time, beating Millwall at White Hart Lane 3-0 (Dalrymple, Parker and McFadden). For the second time they finished fourth, many points behind the champions Derby. Richard McFadden had proved himself up front, breaking Bill Martin's previous best by hitting 18 League goals for the term. The forwards had found better form this year, hitting 61 goals—the best so far.

In 12/3 Orient made an even better beginning. They beat Preston 1-0. 21,000 were at Millfields when Scott and Dalrymple made it 2-0 over Burnley. They shipped Stockport 4-1 (McFadden 2, Dalrymple, Bevan) and went top of the League, six points from three matches. (A new nickname for them at this time was 'The Pearls'; it didn't stick.) But after November they slid out of the top four and finished in 14th position, managing only 34 goals and 10 wins. Sunderland, division champions, beat us 6-0 in the Cup and went on to their second consecutive final. McFadden again headed the scorers with 10. Parker was the only one to appear in every match, and had now become a favourite with the crowd.

Again, the only thing that lost them promotion in 13/4 was their away performance—2 wins, 9 goals in all. They won every game on the home pitch, which pleased the Millfields regulars. Even so they finished 6th, for which the defence must take much of the credit. And they did better in the Cup, drawing at home to Nott'm Forest 2-2 and winning the replay 1-0 with Bowers in goal. But in the next round they went out 3-1 to non-League Brighton. Yet again McFadden topped the scorers with 16 League and 12 Cup goals.

THE FIRST WAR

The 14/5 season was completed in a very halfhearted fashion. The O's maintained their home record with performances like the 3-1 victory over Lincoln and beating Arsenal for the second year running, 1-0. But the full force of the situation was driven home towards the close of the season when an AA gun was moved into Spion Kop at Millfields. The team did very well to finish ninth, and McFadden dug himself out a place in the Orient's history as one of their best ever forwards by scoring 21 goals, bettering his own 11/2 record of 18.

'Orient's splendid lead'—that's what the papers were saying of O's lads, quick off the mark to volunteer for Kitchener. 'Orient have given all clubs in the country a splendid lead. Not only players like McFadden, Jonas, Hugall, Parker, Gibson, Dalrymple, but also club chairman Wells-Holland joined up, the largest squad from any single club in the country. They deserve the best patronage anyone can possibly give. Well done indeed Clapton Orient Football Club.' Orient had now to play in the London temporary A Combination. Every club's gate declined alarmingly, and players' wages, not high before the war, were at a minimum. Fewer players were available. Billy Holmes fetched people in from outside, like Nils Middleboe the Danish international, and amateurs like Ron Blundell. The O's battled on. Hind, Hillsdon and Nightingale had matches and

Hillsdon scored some good goals. Layton still played for a while, and Davis, Goodwin, Dalrymple and Hugall were still there. Jimmy Hugall was the first player to enlist in the Footballers Battalion, becoming a lieutenant. One of the bitterest losses was Richard McFadden, killed in action having won the DCM—a great loss to Clapton Orient and to the game.

After the war, when the first new League season was drawing close, many people praised the Orient, as did the press: 'Good Luck to Clapton Orient. No club has paid a greater price to patriotism than they have.' For the resumption they would miss several former players, though Billy Holmes was still manager, and former centre forward Fred Bevan was made trainer. Their first decade in League football completed, there were now signs that they would go forward in search of the top honours. A number of new men were signed. The brothers Tonner (Sam, Jack and J. E.), John Townrow, and Owen Williams were all fine captures. The start of the 19/20 season was tough, but it was good to see some spectators on Spion Kop again. The next few years saw the O's climb up to hold the top of the table spot briefly, a new stand, the ends of some great careers, and new additions to build up an even finer team—a new lease of life.

Over the season they let in 59, scoring 51, gaining 38 points and finishing fifteenth.

The 20/1 season was better in all departments. The team only conceded a goal a game on average and at Millfields the crowd saw the visiting teams score only nine times in all the 21 matches. They hovered around the top four in the table all season, going into first place on 22nd October, but they couldn't maintain this and finished below the top four. On the 30th April the Prince of Wales visited the Orient at Lea Bridge and saw them beat Notts County 3-0. He was very impressed, and later the Duke of York came. During the summer Orient went on their first ever tour abroad, to Denmark. In the Cup they beat Port Vale in a replay but lost to Bradford 1-0. The reserves were beaten in the final of the London Challenge Cup 1-0 by Crystal Palace.

Always the defence had contributed to any improvement in the team's record, and in the new season 21/2 this was even more so, and much of the interest was centred around the arrival of new goalie Arthur Wood from Southampton. Here was an exciting player if ever there was one. He was inexperienced but opposing teams found it difficult to move much past him, mainly because of his size, and how the crowd loved him. Up front signings Rennox and Percy Whipp added punch to the attack. Owen Williams was in great form and netted 6 in the season, Whipp (before his transfer)

CLAPTON ORIENT F.C., 1921-1922.

scored 8, Rennox leading the list with 11, and at the end they were in 15th position on 39 points.

In February 22 Billy Holmes, the manager for 15 years, died. It was a sad loss; Billy was only 47. He played full back for Orient from 05-13, several times as player-manager.

Things took a swing the other way in the new season, downward. There was undoubted talent and potential but even so, and despite the new manager Fred Powell leading the team from the side, and new signings like Bertie Bliss from Spurs as a replacement for Whipp, there were still problems up front, and when they came dangerously near the relegation zone the dashing lieutenant Jacques of the RAF was called upon, and scored some vital goals. They came desperately close to dropping a division. The final places were: Orient 36 points, Stockport 36, Rotherham 35 and Wolves 27, and the club's position at the close was nineteenth; J. Tonner and Williams scored 7 each, and Bliss 6. The brightest spot was Williams' England cap. The outside left was Orient's first full cap, and played against Wales and Ireland.

In 23/4 there came a great step forward in over-all performance, under new manager Peter Proudfoot. The talking point of the season was goalie Wood. Surely, here was the best uncapped keeper in England. The England keepers at the time were Taylor of Huddersfield and Sewell of Blackburn Rovers. Many thought Wood could have proved better, but he was never capped. Orient finished tenth; just a few more goals could have meant promotion.

It was in this, the 23/4 term that the new stand was opened at Millfields, costing £30,000. On the sad side news that live-wire centre forward Jacques had been killed in an air crash. Early in 1922 the evergreen entertainer Fred Parker said goodbye to the club. Parker had been doing his stuff for over a decade; few would forget bald headed

Fred's sense of fun. The reserve keeper Guy Dale, who came to the club in 1919 died in a motor accident. In 22/3 we had the unique combination of three sets of brothers playing for the two teams: Bob and Jack Duffas, Sam and Jack Tonner and Tom and Owen Williams. There was the death of Billy Holmes. 21/2 was veteran Jimmy Hugall's last season.

THE UNUSUAL TRANSFER OF ALBERT PAPE

In 24/5 Pape had been playing very well at centre forward, coming from Notts County. On 7th February, 25 he had been with the team travelling down to play at Manchester United. Just before the match

he was transferred to United and played for them against Orient, and in fact scored as part of their 4-2 victory. This transfer was a sensation. There had been nothing like it in the history of the League, and Pape's name has come to be remembered for it. Even then he finished Orient's top scorer. In the Cup they lost 1-0 away to Nott'm Forest, but finished in a comfortable position in the League, averaging a goal a game and winning six away matches. As well as Pape's goals Bliss, Hannaford and Rennox scored 5 each. There were no full cap honours but Charlie Hannaford was picked for the FA Commonwealth tour to Australia. Townrow played for an English XI v The Rest at Manchester and earlier for the South v North at Stamford Bridge. South winning 3-0. Arthur Wood represented South Professionals v South Amateurs at Highbury.

One thing overshadowed all else in the 25/6 season—the splendid Cup run in round three, Orient's round of entry, they had a good 1-0 win at Chesterfield (who were riding high in the northern section of the Football League). In round four they beat Middlesborough at Millfields Road. This really aroused the interest in and around Clapton. The next round brought famous Newcastle United to Orient. In their team was the one and only Hughie Gallacher, a small but brilliant centre forward, but it made little difference to the O's who were on the crest of a wave. They won 2-0 with goals from Galbraith and Henderson, in front of over 65,000 overjoyed supporters. In the sixth round Manchester City came to Millfields Road and in front of another very big gate they beat us 6-1. But the Cup had added a great boost to all O's fans.

Our centre-half John Townrow, was capped twice for England this season, against Scotland and Wales. John was mainly selected to mark out Newcastle's Gallacher. He also represented the FL team, and was a great favourite with the supporters. In the League Orient were having a good time— they stayed in third place right up to the end of the year. But then they suffered a number of injuries to key players and just struggled clear of relegation in twentieth position. And this was the season in which the new offside law was introduced, making life a lot easier for forwards.

There were quite a few changes for the 26/7 season. In came Peter Corkindale, a slim, fast winger with a powerful shot, when he felt like having a go, and a new signing from Manchester City, Bob Dennison, a strong attacking forward, but with all these newcomers we still struggled badly, especially the defence. They let in 96 goals. The more Cock, Dennison, Gardner and Corkindale excelled up front, it seemed, the more goalie Wood was picking the ball out of the net. At the finish we had to win the last match, at Reading, and Darlington had to drop a point at Chelsea. Chelsea equalised 40 seconds from time, and Gardner saved our bacon with a penalty, the only goal of the match. They didn't get much closer than that. In the Cup we lost 5-1 away at Port Vale in a replay.

The club's outlook was none too rosy, and manager Proudfoot was hoping for better things in the coming season. For a while it did look as if his dreams would come true, because by October 27 the team actually headed the division, ahead of Manchester City and Chelsea, but fell away so badly that they only just escaped relegation for the third season running. Early in the season the Clapton Stadium Syndicate put forward a plan for dog racing at Millfields Road; they went ahead, spending £80,000, and racing began at Easter. This was a time when we needed loyal staff members, and luckily we had them, in the club secretary Mr. C. W. H. Dean, and trainer Fred Powell, and manager Proudfoot. Towards the close it was rumoured that Peter Proudfoot was a little unsettled in his capacity as O's chief. Results like the good 2-0 win over Barnsley in February, Barnsley having the previous week knocked Fulham for eight, were only smooth spots on a bumpy downhill run.

ANNIVERSARY RELEGATION

It came as no surprise. For the last three seasons their final placing was third from bottom. This time there was no escape. They started with what looked like a good team but things soon went wrong. Another difficulty was the greyhound track encroaching on parts of the pitch. Towards the end of the season bustling forward Turnbull started to slow up and was replaced by new signing Reg Tucker, and winger Charlie Hannaford came back to the side, though he could never replace in-form Corkindale. On the bright side, full back Morely was awarded another cap for the Welsh national team. Turnbull led the scorers list with 13.

With the League performances casting a gloom over Millfields it was a relief when the Cup came along. Drawing Southampton gave Arthur Wood a chance to play on the ground he left eight years ago. The club were now division 2 promotion contenders, but we held them to a goalless draw. Wood blocking everything. The replay at Millfields Road was an exciting one, and O's won 2-1, a fine performance. Then they drew Aston Villa in round four, one of the finest teams in the country, and the most prolific goalscorers in the top two divisions —everybody wrote off the O's, but they made a supreme effort and drew the match 0-0. The replay on the 30th January was a different story. Villa changed their left wing pair, Orient stayed the same. Villa went ahead and then piled in the goals, the final result 8-0 to Villa. Orient did not deserve to lose by this margin but after the third goal went in they visibly sank. Aston Villa are the only team ever to score 8 goals against the O's before or after.

Arthur Grimsdell took over the job of player-manager for the 29/30 season in division three, optimistic of a quick return. He brought in new faces into the team like bright young prospect, Tommy Mills, and

T. Mills,
International 1933, *v* Ireland and England.

win through Mills and Grimsdell. They beat Bristol Rovers, from our own division, 1-0 at home. Then, in the fourth round, they drew Newcastle United, Orient put up a spirited show but went down 3-1. Mills scored our goal and J. Richardson, who became trainer with Orient in later years, made a hat-trick for Newcastle. Later on, Wales honoured a splendid right-back Morely with caps against England and Scotland. Edmonds finished top scorer with 13 goals; 55 goals in all gave us 41 points, and the twelfth position. One of the only good things about the drop into division three was that the travel expenses were considerably reduced. Already, by March 30 arrangements had been made for Orient to move to Lea Bridge, (a FL commission had viewed the new headquarters favourably).

A YEAR OF CRISIS: MOVE TO LEA BRIDGE STADIUM

After the loss of Millfields to greyhound racing the team struggled in the 30/1 season. It was sad, because the club had made enormous ground improvements—all told it was a heavy burden on the finances. Lea Bridge Speedway was just half a mile away.

The new home was rather bleak, though it could hold quite a large crowd. Soon after the move came one of the best wins of the season, 4-0 against Torquay. Torquay objected to the fence being too near the touchline, and on inspection FL officials ordered Orient to correct this and alter the pitch dimensions slightly.

ORIENT AT WEMBLEY

In the meantime, where were the O's to play? Well, with the League's permission, Clapton Orient went to Wembley. On 22nd November, 30 we beat Brentford 3-0 there, and on 6th December Southend 3-1—a pity more games weren't played there. Back at Lea Bridge visitors Norwich and Walsall only drew 3-4,000 fans. The financial position

new forwards Rollo Jack and Sid Hoar. Players who left included Gardner, Kerr and McDonald. Arthur Woods was gradually declining, but he still played more matches than the other keepers. The first ever match in the new division was against Plymouth Argyle, and we lost 2-0 in front of 19,700, though over the year they did well. They had a fine Cup run too, starting off in the first round proper against non-League Folkestone Town. They were held to a goalless draw and in the replay were held again 2-2. The third match was played at Highbury, Orient winning easily 4-1 with goals from Eastman, Vanner, Campbell and player-manager Grimsdell. Another non-League club, Northfleet, caused us no trouble—a 2-0 of the club was again at rock bottom. Four M.P.'s, F. C. Watkins, Herbert Morrison, H. W. Wallace and A. M. Hudson, sent the club a letter in which they appealed to all football lovers to help Orient over their troubles by contributing to a 50,000 shilling fund. They each put a pound in to start the ball rolling. There were supporters meetings at Hackney Town Hall, dances and concerts at St. Jane's Hall and Kings Hall. More meetings at the 'White Hart', Devonshire Hall and The 'George' in Glyn Road, and a supporters night at the Walthamstow Palace, etc., etc. In February we were forced to sell veteran Galbraith to Cardiff City to make ends meet, but despite gloomy rumours the club was still above water at the close of the term. Orient and their fans had fought bitterly against heavy odds. Arthur Wood made his last appearance, the 374th, an all time record, when the team beat Luton Town 3-2 on 18th April. And that day Jimmy Seed took over from Peter Proudfoot as manager. In the Cup they went out to Luton at home 4-2 after forcing a 2-2 draw away. Tricker was top scorer on 18. People expected a lot from Jimmy Seed (who, incidentally, changed the colours from the famous white with red V to red and white hooped shirts and black shorts), and the forwards did hit 77 goals in 31/2, but the defence conceded 90, and the final placing was sixteenth on 35 points.

The financial state of the club was causing grave concern, and eventually an official receiver-manager was appointed. The rumour of merger with Thames FC, also struggling in the third division, was dismissed. Their gates were even lower than ours, which were 7,000 on average. People who gave the club grand assistance in their hour of need were: Orient chairman, P. Boydin, and supporters club officials, S. Holman, T. Halsey, T. Peters and many others. St. James Hall in Clapton became the weekly scene for functions and meetings in an effort to raise cash. They were hoping for a good run in the Cup, but, having beaten Coventry in

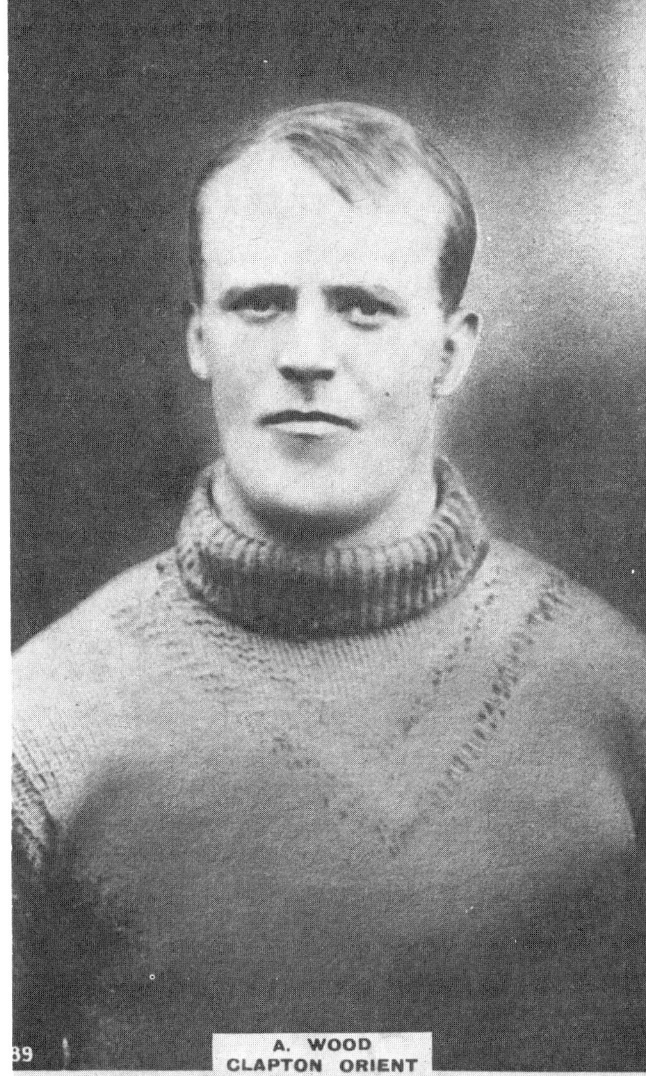

the first round they went out at 4-0 at Cardiff.

Altogether they used 28 players in the 31/2 squad. For the next season Jimmy Seed brought ex-internationals Stan Earle and Jimmy Dimmock to play for the side as well as signing twelve other players. After nine matches only two had been lost but only two won, making five draws. From then on, the defeats became more regular.

MONEY CRISIS YET AGAIN

Lack of success reduced the gates, and in November the FA ordered that unless certain debts were paid by December 1st the membership of the club might be withdrawn. The club's resources were so depleted, this looked as though it was the end— certainly Orient's worst money crisis yet. A set of amateur players stood by to play for the O's. Then director Snewin's phone rang. A Mr. Phillips promised a cheque for £400. Mr. Snewin and manager Seed went along to Godfrey Phillips' factory, and a Mr. Arthur Phillips handed over the cheque, with the promise of more to come. Mr. Phillips, a Clapton man explained that certain football pool money raised at his factory, if not won, could go Orient's way as he had always been interested in the club since a small boy. The professional team celebrated this good Samaritan act by beating Watford 2-0 at Lea Bridge. Just prior to the money crisis Orient met Aldershot in a Cup-tie on 26th November at home in the first round, losing in a hard fought game 1-0. The second part of the season was a real battle, and re-election was only avoided on goal average; Newport County and Swindon just saving the day, all three on 29 points. Just prior to Christmas many schemes and ideas were discussed by directors, officials and supporters, including a share scheme; the money problems had by no means been solved by the end of the season. Tricker once more topped the charts with 14 goals —in all 59, the lowest in the division.

David Pratt became the manager for the 33/3 season and he seemed to bring a breath of fresh air into the club. On 10th February they chalked up a record score, hammering Aldershot 9-2. The majority of clubs were now finding Orient's forwards difficult to handle. The side moved so sweetly at times; Halliday was a brilliant leader. Rigby at outside left was shrewd; Tommy Mills played with rare skill, and on the right wing was Mayson, one of the fastest movers Orient ever had. Inside right was the powerful Ted Crawford. This was the first season since 23/4 in which they scored more than they conceded. Yet their away performances still let them down, and they finished in eleventh place. The FA Cup draw gave Orient an interesting round at home to Epsom Town, and what a gallant fight they put up, but our skills and experience were a bit too much for the amateurs, Orient winning 4-2. They then drew Walsall away and held them to a goalless draw. In the replay they mastered the Midlands Club winning 2-0. There were jibes made at the Walsall players by Orient fans after the match, "We 'aint Arsenal you know". Walsall had knocked the Gunners out of the cup the season before. So they had marched on into round three with a tough draw away at Grimsby Town. Grimsby were having a fine season and eventually romped away with the division 2 title, scoring 103 goals in the process; yet Orient went to Blundell Park and looked every bit as good, only going down 1-0. And at last, this season, clever forward Tommy Mills was awarded a Welsh international cap, against England. Playing for us since 1929 he had quite a following and richly deserved his honour, (he went to Leicester for the new season).

Orient dropped three places during the 34/5 season. Mills had left for a large, welcome fee, and manager Pratt then signed Vince Farrell from Everton, and Harold Taylor to fill Mills' position. Some exciting matches were seen in the season. Orient's best League victory was the 6-0 win over Brighton, yet they soon hit a bad patch with five consecutive defeats. In the FA Cup they were drawn at non-League Ashford Town. Orient were too strong for the home club winning 4-1. In round two they were home to Chester, a top team in the northern section of division three. And in a keenly fought tie the Cheshire club won 3-1. In the new year manager David Pratt left the club. The fans were greatly disappointed and raised a petition, though nothing came of it. The ever reliable trainer, S. White took over temporarily. By February the finances were very nearly at crisis proportions again, and two directors

had left, taking bank guarantees of £700. On the football side they made it through the year, safe in fourteenth place, scoring 46 goals and letting through 46.

In the 35/6 season back came player manager Peter Proudfoot. They opened at home to Luton on 31st August, beating Hatters 3-0, with new players in the side. Dave Affleck was at centre-half, a tall young Scotsman from Ayrshire who turned out to be the discovery of the season, and his 6ft and 13 stone certainly helped at the back. The team followed up with a 1-0 win over Reading, but unfortunately they suffered five away defeats at the start.

CRAWFORD'S GOALSCORING RECORD

A memorable feature of the season was the goalscoring of big centre forward Ted Crawford. He netted 23 goals, thus creating a new individual Orient record, breaking McFadden's record of 21 during the 14/5 season. Another feature was the fine FA Cup run. In the first round they had to travel to Aldershot, which ended goalless. In the replay at Lea Bridge, they won 1-0 with Crawford getting the all important goal. The second round saw them drawn away to non-Leaguers Folkestone, and they won 2-1 with goals from McAleer and Crawford. So on to round three, a home tie against Charlton Athletic, who were right on top of the second division, having a great twenty match unbeaten spell, but the O's put an end to that. They slammed Charlton 3-0. Acrobatic Charlton goalkeeper Sam Bartram couldn't stop them marching into round four, with an away tie at first division Middlesborough. We were beaten 3-0, but did rather well over all considering three of the ties were away from home. They finished in fourteenth position in the League, scoring 55 goals.

PROMOTION SEEMED NO NEARER

This was the eighth season in the third division (south); there had to be a lot more signings. The player who held most attention

CLAPTON ORIENT F.C.   1935-36.

E. Ware   V. Farrell   D. Affleck   G. Woods

S. E. White (Trainer)   W. Trodd   G. Heinemann   F. Searle   D. Wall   C. Hilam   G. Pateman   B. Herod   J. Taylor   W. Wright (Asst. Trainer)

P. Proudfoot (Manager)   R. Quinn   G. Reed   H. Smith   A. Hurst   E. Edwards   J. Mayson   V. Hammond   E. Crawford   T. W. Halsey (Secretary)

L. Caiels   H. Campbell   W. Fogg   I. Miles   H. Taylor   T. Foster

was centre-half Dave Affleck; he had a fine season—so much so he was transferred to Southampton, a pity because he became a firm favourite with the fans. Orient had one of the best defences in the League. They were a hard nut to crack and had only 52 goals hit past them. It was the forwards who let us down; just a bit more punch up front would have seen the Orient promoted.

In February Frank Snewin, the chairman, described the rumour of a move to Mitcham as preposterous. The O's must stay in the area to keep faith with the fans. And, in fact, talks were in progress with Leyton council about the difficulty Leyton amateurs were having in paying the rent on their Brisbane Road ground. Orient made a bid for the ground, and soon everything was signed and sealed, the move to be made in time for the start of the new season. Back at Lea Bridge Orient were proving difficult to beat. They went from September until March unbeaten. Jack Smith who came to us in October, finished the season as captain and coach to the reserves, who were struggling in the London Combination. The first team were finally placed twelfth (Crawford 12 goals). In the Cup they beat Torquay 2-1 but crashed in the second round 4-1 to Carlisle.

FIRST GAME AT BRISBANE ROAD

Perhaps the new surroundings took some getting used to? Whatever it was, the 37/8 season did not come up with the answers to the club's problems. Brisbane Ground, Leyton was just off the High Road, (it also was known as the Osborne Road ground).

The ground had scope for improvement. Some parts were primitive: there was only one small stand, affectionately known as 'the orange box', seating about 475 spectators. Beside this on one side was a large grassy hill. The ends behind each goal were not too bad, but were mainly cinders under foot. A white fence surrounded the pitch.

The west stand (standing) held a lot of people, it wasn't a little ground; the only trouble was we did not own it, but rented it from the Leyton council.

14,598 came to the big kick off there on 28th August, 1937, against Cardiff City. The result was tied 1-1. Fred Tully scored the goal and Charlie Hillam was playing his 100th match for the club. They struggled all season finishing fourth from bottom with only 33 points, 3 points clear of Torquay United. Not one of Orient's 21 away games was drawn; they took 6 points from their away trips and suffered 18 defeats (the most Orient have ever lost during a season). The club again stated that they were in financial difficulty; officials had to scotch a silly rumour that the players were receiving no wages, with a statement to the local press. During the season manager Proudfoot was assisted by trainer Bill Wright and secretary Tom Halsey. The supporters club appointed a new secretary, a Mr. Jack Insole, son of the famous cricketer Doug. In the Cup they beat Torquay United in the first round 2-1 with goals from Tully and Graham. The next round saw a home tie against York City; the teams battled out a 2-2 draw (Lane and H. Smith). In the replay we went out 1-0 at York. Over all we scored 42 goals, conceded 61.

Now it was ten years since the club suffered relegation. We have seen many good players come and go, a number of managers, and a lot of high hopes. Each season saw a struggle to avoid the bottom of the table. In 39 they finished twentieth, scored 53 and let in only 55 goals. There were more departures, like goalkeeper Hillam who played in 125 matches and Fred Searle, who made 122 appearances. Some new blood had been brought in, and the team received some glowing reports, like the match at Swindon, where their movements with five forwards in a line were a delight to watch. And they became known as a great sporting side. In the Cup they had to take on sprightly amateurs Hayes in the first round, winning 3-1. In round two they were drawn at Walsall, losing in front of 13,570, 4-2; the scorers were Crawford and Williams. During the season Peter Proudfoot retired through ill health and secretary Tom Halsey was appointed to take his place. Proudfoot had a long association with Orient as player and manager. Ron Williams (signed from West Ham) was top scorer on 17 and scored in his own benefit match against Millwall.

THE SECOND WAR

There were good new recruits for the start of the 39/40 season. Manager Halsey made some clever transactions: J. Ellis, a goalkeeper from Hull City, J. Turner from Bristol City, R. Bungay from Mansfield Town, and R. Ranson from Bournemouth. One of the most exciting signings was that of Scottish forward W. McFayden from Huddersfield Town (a few years earlier he hit 52 goals in 34 matches for Motherwell). Also signed was Les Gore, a future manager, from Bradford City, amongst other forwards. They also retained eleven of their 38/9 squad, and it was thought that at last, here, they had a group of players who could challenge for promotion to Division 2. The season got under way at home to Ipswich Town on 26th August, 39, and with such a string of players Halsey had a headache trying to pick a team. It was a nice one, though, and they drew 2-2, Gore and Williams getting the goals. 11,018 came to cheer them on.

The unrest, the headlines—World War Two was not entirely unexpected. All Orient's hopes (and everyone elses) really were gone now. Once again, immediately this time, the League had to be suspended. Wartime regional competitions were started, the clubs using amateur and guest players, and were not taken too seriously. What with the club being in Leyton for a couple of years now, they were often called just Orient, though still officially Clapton Orient.

After the War

During 40/1 the gates went down to around the 1,000 mark, and many players guested for us. 41/2 was tough and army service took away most of the players. Manager Bill Wright even turned out a couple of times. The strip was changed to white shirts and black shorts; red and white hoops were felt to be too bright for the times. The same situation continued during 42/3. In 43/4 Trevor Ford guested for us, later becoming famous in the Aston Villa side and as a Welsh international. He also played for Orient in 44/5 and in this year the team changed their colours once more, this time back to the well known white shirts with the big red V and black shorts. By 44 the crowds were up around the 8,000 mark, results often tended to be farcical owing to the difficulty in fielding teams.

Even during the 45/6 season League soccer was not resumed owing to players returning from overseas, but the FA Cup, on a two leg basis, was back. It was a period of adjustment for professional clubs. Orient were drawn against Newport, Isle of Wight in the FA Cup first round, and Newport won the replay 2-0 and the round 3-2 on aggregate.

Orient tried many guest players that year; Alec Stock (QPR) and Campbell (Raith Rovers) were two of the better known. Tragically, in his fourth month as manager, Hall was taken seriously ill, and loyal Bill Wright had to come in again. Without him the club would have been forced to close up during the war years. Two of Hall's signings were army forward Wally Pullin and halfback J. Pullbrook. Among the regulars reappearing were: Hall, Ringrose, Bart-lett, Howshall, Gore, Farley and also the ageing Fletcher. The brightest spot was when the reserves won the FL Combination Cup, beating Fulham reserves 3-1 on West Ham's ground.

The first full League programme after seven year wartime regionalised Leagues wasn't too successful under new manager and secretary Captain Charles Hewitt. He was looking to the future; his motto was: 'The best is good enough for the club.' He had plans for a full-size pitch, with a grass verge which could be built into a running-track, new stands with tip-up seats (everything in steel and concrete), refreshment bars and accommodation for 70,000 fans. But first, he set about the team. He saw that most of the old pre-war squad needed replacing. Hewitt's best discovery was left-back Ledger Ritson, he was small but a grafter, with a touch of class.

NAME CHANGED TO LEYTON ORIENT

After forty years the club changed its name to Leyton Orient Football Club. This was announced at the match versus Crystal Palace on Wednesday 2nd October, 46. Councillors of the borough, and former players of the Orient were at the match. The Mayor of Leyton wasn't able to attend although he did send the following message to the chairman Dr. A. J. Byrne and the rest of the board:

"It gives me great pleasure to learn recently of the official change in name of your club to Leyton Orient FC Ltd., and I should like to take this opportunity of sending you my very best wishes on this memorable occasion. I trust the incorporation of the borough's name in your title may mark the beginning of a period of continued and well deserved success. With every good wish for your future. Yours very truly, A. Crown."

Good wishes were also received from many others.

On the 12th October manager Charles Hewitt was set to sign a young northern player, by the 16th the deal was off. There had been an unspecified hitch. The board met, and on the 20th Hewitt resigned, and William Bulloch Wright took over. But very soon Hewitt was invited back, this time to become secretary and general manager. Wright was to be assistant manager, and R. Hollo Jack assistant secretary. All was not yet well at the O's.

Worse was to follow. On the field the team by this time were struggling and by the end of November had gained only two wins from twelve games. Orient by this time were in more financial difficulty and the supporters club, a voluntary subsidiary of the football club, controlled by a management committee, set up a £4000 'fighting fund' for the club to battle its way back to the League table. Hewitt made it known that he had tried to sign many players but without much success. He also placed on record through the club programme the services rendered to the club by the new club chairmen Mr. F. W. Snewin, G. S. Harris and H. F. Robertson. "For years these three have shouldered a heavy financial burden, and those interested in the welfare of the club owe to them at least a deep measure of gratitude. Mr. Snewin in particular has advanced large sums of money to keep the Orient flag flying. But for these three men the O's would have become submerged. A former mayor of Hackney, Mr. Snewin has played a worthy part in public affairs. He is full of enthusiasm for the future and hopes to see the O's going places."

They certainly were not let down by the players, who just avoided the drop by steering us into nineteenth place with a 2-1 victory at Notts County. Hunt was top scorer on 13, level with Wally Pullen. The supporters club made £1000 all told, and they came up with a new supporters club signature tune, which went something like this:

Let's go along to the Orient, Shoot, Bang,
Goal,
Let's go along to the Orient, Shoot, Bang,
Goal,
Wherever we play, at home or away,
Everyone yells 'Up the O's' so
Let's go along to the Orient,
Shoot, Bang, Goal.

Right at the end of this eventful season it was announced that the shareholders of the club had unanimously elected to the board of directors: Mr. E. W. Girt, Mr. G. S. Kenure, Mr. R. E. Lea and Mr. A. E. Page. It was announced: 'These are gentlemen who will put Orient on the map. They have been working behind the scenes for some time, but much depends upon the result of our desire to purchase from the local corporation the freehold of the ground and buildings thereon.' And on the appointment as director of Arthur Page the following was printed in the programme:

Mr. A. E. Page is another big business executive and is a company director of great repute, and a gentleman farmer resident in Dunmow, Essex. Mr. Page has been an Orient fan from boyhood, and has been a loyal stand patron throughout the years from Millfields to Leyton. Never faltering in his loyalty and devotion to Orient, he has rarely missed a home match, and is cognizant of the long struggle against adversity. Despite everything, Mr. Page is proud to be a director of the club he has always had very much at heart. A very charming and delightful personality, Mr. Page will not rest content until the Orient are in possession of a

Jackie Deverall, a strong midfield player

team and ground second to none in London.

The 47/8 season saw another change in club colours, royal blue shirts and white shorts, and a number of new players, but the team dropped points and were not scoring too many goals, so Hewitt went out and bought big strong Frank Neary from West Ham United. Frank had one of the hardest right-foot shots around. But still they slithered to almost bottom. Just after Christmas it looked a foregone conclusion that they would have to apply for re-election, but the team pulled clear. With something like promotion form they took 25 points from their last sixteen matches. This brought their goal total to 51 and pulled them up to seventeenth position. Neary led the scorers list with 15. In the Cup they were poor, going down to Southern League Gillingham 1-0 on their sloping pitch. Hewitt, who had guided the team well, left the club at the end of the season and Neil McBain took over.

Under McBain the 48/9 term was another hard one. A bid from Birmingham for Ritson was turned down and soon after he broke his leg against Northampton. It turned out to be an unlucky season in this way with nine players in all put out of the side through injury, and McBain was forced to make a lot of signings. What kept the fans happy was the power shooting of Frank Neary. A brace he scored at Walsall (Orient winning 3-2) broke Ted Crawford's scoring record (23, during 35/6 season). Neary finished with 26 goals. Someone not likely to forget Neary's shooting is McFeat the Torquay goalkeeper for, on 20th November 48, in a match at Leyton stadium he was knocked clean out by a tremendous shot from Neary. It was close on half an hour before McFeat could resume in goal.

The best victories came early on. They beat both Newport County and Exeter City 5-2, and Notts County 3-1, Neary getting a hat-trick, his third a vicious 16 yard cross shot that ripped over the goalie's arms into the net. The team must have viewed their FA Cup round one match at Southern League Dartford very cautiously. Dartford took an early lead, but Deverall soon levelled the scores, and in an inspiring spell Connelly and McGeachy saw them through. During April Cyril Bacon passed the total of 100 League appearances for the Orient. On 16th April 49 they were beaten 7-1 at Torquay, the first time they had conceded more than six goals in a League match. (They had conceded 6 goals in a League match on 17 occasions prior to this 48/9 season). Orient finished in lowly nineteenth position, scoring 58 goals and with 34 points. Yet again they had left it mighty close for comfort.

THE CLOSEST SHAVE OF ALL

The start of the 49/50 season saw Harry 'Cigar' Zussman take over the chairmanship of the club. Versatile Wally Pullen scored many goals for the Orient but none more valuable than the one he got at Southend on 6th May, 50. The situation was this: Orient needed at least one point from the match to stand any chance of avoiding re-election; at the same time, Southend needed to win to gain the runners-up place in the table, which meant much more money for the seasiders. The pitch was very muddy after it had rained all morning. There was no score at half-time but soon McEwan put the O's ahead. Southend equalised and with only ten minutes to go, Wakefield put them ahead. It looked all over, and with the minutes ticking away team captain Banner signalled all his men up the field for one last effort. With just 10 seconds left a lob floated into the Southend goal-mouth, Pullen had it with his back to the Southend goal. Somehow he flicked the ball back-wards and into the net, to the cheers of 15,000 fans. Pullen was the hero for Orient that night.

Alec Stock spent his first season as manager building up the side. He signed Sid Hobbins a goalkeeper from Millwall, Jackie Wood from West Ham, and winger Alan Smith from QPR. But perhaps the best new prospects who came to us were George Sutherland from Partick Thistle and young keeper Pat Welton from minor club Chislehurst. Possibly the best performance that season was at Ipswich Town, Sutherland getting a hat-trick. This was one of Frank Neary's last matches for us; he moved to QPR, who were in the second division. Then manager Stock went out and bought Jimmy Blair from Bournemouth, and he played in the return game against Ipswich Town which

Arthur Banner, Captain and defender

we won easily 4-0 and in which George Sutherland again scored a hat-trick. In all Orient's history there cannot be found another player who has scored a hat-trick in both League fixtures against one club home and away. The funny thing about Sutherland was that he wasn't a very skillful player, but what energy, spirit and an eye for goal. He was rather short for a centre forward, but he would chase any ball and a match, for him, was not lost until it was over.

There was always a bit of humour down the O's. For example, Cyril Trailer in a fierce tackle ripped his shorts, and, before he could put on a new pair, a Northampton forward came surging past, but Trailer, with strands of material dangling all round his legs, broke the attack, amid laughter and great applause. He was then free to put on new shorts, and all turned out well because we went on to win 2-0, Sutherland scoring the winner. Orient registered their first away win at Walsall 2-1. They drew against Millwall 1-1, and then won at Swindon 1-0. It was these three matches that kept them safe, in eighteenth place on 53 goals, (Sutherland 16). Neary was transferred very early on in the season—who knows what he would have done if he had stayed? Stock introduced an A team in the Midweek League, and a junior team for the first time in years. The juniors played in black strip and were known as the All Blacks.

During the 50/1 season Stock signed probably the strongest list since David Pratt's ventures in the transfer market in 33. At least it was seen that Orient were thinking big in a bid for an outstanding year. Though they lost their first League match 2-1 at Plymouth, they still made a good start, winning four of their first six games. But the form didn't last and Stock let many players go. Despite all the promise and talent in the team they again finished in a low position, though Stock's later signings, Stan Aldous, Les Blizzard and Willie Robb, were now playing well. They went out 2-1 to Ipswich in the FA Cup on a foggy day in November. They were hit by injuries very badly towards the end of the term, and they particularly lacked a hard-hitting centre forward. A testimonial was held for Ritson at the end and many donations were received, and the club held a benefit for Wally Pullen, though they were still hard up. A plan from Alec Stock for the issue of shares to the public was announced in the following letter:

THIS CONCERNS YOU!!
A PERSONAL MESSAGE FROM MANAGER
ALEC STOCK TO ALL SUPPORTERS

It is the ambition of Leyton Orient FC now, and in the future, to offer, as far as possible, the best—and only the best. For many years now Orient has been under a cloud. At the beginning of this season, as you are well aware, my Directors made an all out effort to put Orient "on the map" and a considerable sum of money was spent in securing the transfers of top-class players. This indeed was a big gamble to take for the Orient with such a limited capital at their disposal, but it was the policy of the Directors and myself to give you loyal Orient supporters something in return for your ardent and faithful support of the old Club. Whether the gamble has been a success or not—I leave that for you to decide, but it is the intention of the Club to continue to offer better football at Leyton Stadium, and to do this necessary steps must be taken to make sacrifices. The burden carried throughout this season by the Directors has been a heavy one, and with current difficulties facts must be faced. Like many other Football League Clubs, Orient feel a financial strain. The Board do not desire to part with our best players in order to meet financial commitments. The policy is to keep the best for the fulfilment of the future.

To do this, I make this personal appeal to you, and ask for your heartfelt co-operation. It has been suggested that the Club float a number of shares at £1 each —a maximum number for holding by one person being five (£5). Would you, as an Orient wellwisher and supporter, be prepared to back us in this movement? We feel that this is the best way out if the Club is to carry on a progressive policy and not part with the best men—a move which would obviously get us nowhere. We are appending below a questionaire on which we would be grateful to have the views of as many of you as possible, as to whether you consider such a proposal worthy of further consideration.

Please let us have your views.

Polish goalkeeper Stan Gerula decided to leave the club to settle in America and play with the Chicago Athletic Football Club.

During the way he played in international games for his country and was a member of the famous Polish team of footballers called the Carpathians. And there honour was the news that assistant manager Joe Edelston was to be awarded a medal for his service to football. On the field Jimmy Blair had a fine season and finished the season as top scorer with 16 goals. He will be remembered for his brilliant ball play, very nimble. With the team quite safe in the table by the end of April, the club staged a Festival of Britain match against Racing Club Haarlem of Holland winning 3-1. A match of this calibre made a fitting windup to the football year.

Before the start of the 51/2 season two former players rejoined the club in other capacities. Jack Tonner, former inside forward from 19/26, returned as head groundsman and Les Gore, winger from 39/46, was appointed assistant trainer. The Orient also adopted junior club, Chase of Chertsey, the former Arsenal club, because the directors had decided to withdraw from the London Midweek League. FC Chase of Chertsey produced some fine players, one, a 17 year old outside right, Brian Jackson, who showed coolness and trickery on the wing, played in 21 matches for the first team. Young Pat Welton made a tremendous improvement in goal for the O's and had the distinction of being the only ever-present player in the campaign. Young players on view in the Orient had their public trial on 11th August 51. Dave Groombridge, formerly with Chase of Chertsey who played for Hayes Athletic in the Amateur Cup against Leytonstone the season before, was wanted by many big League clubs. George Putt was signed

Manager Alex Stock

on a month's trial (a close friend of O's player Taffy Evans). Ernie Stanley aged 23 from the Arsenal, who played cricket for Essex during the summer was there, Bert Hawkins, a big centre forward came from Gravesend and Northfleet in the Southern League; he had been the top scorer in that League for the past three seasons. Joe Steele came from Bury, where he made 25 appearances, Paddy Blatchford from Plymouth Argyle. Jimmy Richardson was made first team trainer, and the local council and the supporters club had given money to erect a new wall around the ground to replace the familiar white fence. The scene was set for the start of 51/2.

The first game was at home to Plymouth

Argyle, Orient coming out on top 1-0 (Rees the scorer), then on to Watford where they obtained their second successive win 1-0. They continued to play well and soon found themselves second in the table. Not to be outdone the youth team, Chase of Chertsey went to San Remo to play in an international tournament and reached the final, losing to Barcelona by a lone goal. So far so good for the first team, with eleven points from seven games and challenging the leaders Plymouth Argyle. Then, towards the end of September they began to slip, and when this continued Stock decided to sell winger Brian Jackson to Liverpool in exchange for Des Woan, a 23 year old forward.

THE GREAT CUP RUN

On 24th November they played the first Cup-tie, against Eastern Counties League side Gorleston, a match all fans thought would be a walkover for Orient, but they were wrong. Gorleston, in their usual green shirts, held us to a 2-2 draw. For the replay they brought in Deverall and Bert Hawkins, and with defences mostly on top, it ended all square at 0-0. And so to a third tie, to be played at Arsenal. Alec Stock was a little worried by the lack of finish up front so he decided to bring in young Dennis Pacey only just signed from Walton and Hersham, he was a 6ft 3in long legged lad and he could really hit a ball. Many fans queried 'Who's Pacey?' They were soon to find out. He slammed a hat-trick in his very first match, Orient winning a grand game 5-4. So to the next round at Wrexham, where they earned a replay back in London on 19th December, and it was a splendid match. With only six minutes to go in extra time, Pacey nodded in to the goalmouth and the lively Rees headed the winner, 3-2.

The third round they took second division Everton to a replay. For the replay Rees was missing and Tommy Harris took his place, and in the 64th minute Pacey

▲ *John 'Taffy' Evans, a popular defender*
◄ *Tommy Brown, a reliable midfield player*

broke loose to slam in number three for 'giant killers' Orient. The fourth round took us to Birmingham, top of the second division and the team pulled off a fine victory by 1-0 at St. Andrews. For the two matches at Everton and Birmingham City, Orient borrowed the Arsenal's shirts of red with white sleeves and it turned out a funny twist of fate. They were drawn at home to the Gunners in the fifth round on 23rd February 52. A crowd of just over 30,000 saw the match and Arsenal were just that bit too strong, winning 3-0. The terracing behind the Coronation Gardens had been specially improved for the match and the club over the past few weeks had received much needed publicity and money. Orient, in fact, were the most discussed and envied team in the country during their famous Cup run. Young goalkeeper Dave Groombridge looked likely to press Welton hard for a first team place next season; he played five matches this term. In the League the team slipped down to finish in a lowly eighteenth position on 41 points, scoring a total of 55 goals. Pacey scored 17 League and Cup goals followed by Rees with 16. Stan Aldous played in every game, 55 League and Cup. After such a good Cup year the supporters were hoping for something special from the team during the 52/3 season and there was good material. There was the new amateur right-back Stan Charlton. The 22 year old ex-Bromley player who later in the season was due to leave the army, turned out to be a big favourite with the fans especially for his now famous sliding tackle. Stan was a member of the British team for the Olympic Games in Helsinki. Also playing well that day was new captain Stan Aldous and in goal Pat Welton brought off some great saves. Alex Stock had brought a few new faces to the club during the close season, namely: Sid Bishop, another of the Chase of Chertsey players, Cliff Mansley from Preston, Ken Facey who wasn't really a newcomer, and

Forward Jimmie Blair ▲

Winger Brian Jackson ▶

Centre half Stan Aldous captained Orient's 55/6 promotion team

Ron Foster, serving in the forces and another Chase of Chertsey player. Selwyn Jones signed from Sheffield Wednesday and George Poulton came from Gillingham.

Soon after, against Torquay United, Dennis Pacey found his form. Firstly he jumped up to nod us into the lead, then scored another. George Poulton, making his League debut, knocked in two more; goalkeeper Dave Groombridge was hardly bothered at all and Orient eventually won 4-1. They then caned QPR 5-0. It seemed to be a thrill-a-week. Jimmy Scarth of Gillingham scored a hat-trick in 2.5 minutes to beat the

quickest scoring hat-trick held by Billy Lane (also against Orient) in 1933, though we did pull two back through Poulton and Niblett. Orient's 1-1 draw with Reading was a memorable one for Ken Facey. The Berkshire lads were winning with only four minutes left and Facey, in his home League debut, scored with a great header to the delight of his team mates. At this time the team were lying in a worrying third from bottom position, but after beating Southend 3-0 with goals from Pacey, Poulton and Brown, they began to move up the table and by the close had reached a comfortable half way position.

Before the end of the season the club had a meeting to discuss the issue of shares. They issued £20,000 at 5/- a share to the public in an effort to raise some capital. Even with money problems, the club still held testimonials for Arthur Banner and Jackie Deverall late on in the season and many famous names turned out for Banner, like Tommy Harmer (Spurs), Eddie Bailey (Spurs), Cox (Arsenal) and Gray (Chelsea). Soon after he was appointed player-manager of Sittingbourne. In the Cup the team couldn't match last season's great run, going out to Bristol Rovers after a replay. Mr. Joe Edelston, the assistant manager, who had given such service to the club, was forced to leave because of ill health. The club were honoured by amateur David 'Dai' Davies playing for Harwich and Parkeston in the FA Amateur Cup final; he was on loan to them and mainly played for Orient's reserves. They weren't having such a good season; their best win was 8-2 over Aldershot reserves. A sad feature was the departure of player-manager Jimmy Blair to Ramsgate. He made a total of 107 League appearances, a fine servant to the club.

For the first time since 25/6 Orient now reached the Cup sixth round. On 21st November 53 they comfortably beat Southern League Kettering 3-0 with goals from Poulton 2, and Ken Facey. The next round saw them drawn at home again to a Southern League side, Weymouth, Orient revealing themselves masters as soon as the game started, and we went on to hit four goals, from Rees 2, Morgan and Pacey. Morgan, an experienced halfback, was one of Stock's shrewd close season buys, from Southampton. He also signed centre forward Stan Edwards (once with Chelsea) from Colchester, and clever winger Phil White from Wealdstone. In round three they made the long journey from Tranmere. Nearly 1000 fans travelled to cheer the Orient on. But they had an early shock, and Ken Facey equalised only through a penalty. So it was all back to Brisbane Road on the Thursday. Stock decided to play Billy Rees even though he wasn't fully fit. Soon after the interval Pacey ran from nowhere to slide home Morgan's great pass. After that there was no stopping them. Rees and Pacey added further goals, and Pacey hit home number four (his hat-trick) to put Tranmere out 4-1.

For round four we were drawn at home to Fulham, who had made heavy weather of beating Grimsby. Stock brought in 'Dai' Davies at centre forward, Moragn had a good effort saved, and after five minutes we took the lead and when reserve 'Dai' Davies headed number two and the 30,000 all-ticket crowd went wild with delight. So, as in the 52/3 season Stock's gamble, playing a young forward in an important Cup-tie, paid off. In the Fulham side on that day were Johnny Haynes, Jimmy Hill, Badford Jezzard and Bobby Robson.

Some people thought Orient were making a large profit out of this Cup success. They didn't stop to think of the varied channels which drain off money at every Cup-tie. Manager Stock issued the following financial survey of the match with Fulham:

Gross gate money	£3481
Entertainment Tax	743
Police	48
Gatemen, referee, linesmen, printing and	

Goalie Pat Welton saved many penalties

postage	120
Fulham FC expenses	15
Share to Fulham	851
Share to FA Cup pool	851
FL 40% Levy	34
Incidental expenses: special training, crash barriers, etc.	—
Net Gain	819

In the next round they made a great comeback to beat Doncaster at the stadium, and even the most sober minded (strictly impartial) members of the Press had to give vent to their feelings of admiration. It was a moving experience to walk down Leyton High Road on the morning of the sixth round match against Port Vale. It seemed that almost every shop carried a "Good Luck Orient" message on their window and some shops and garages had very elaborate good wish decorations. Port Vale, leaders of the third division, were a very defensive side, and so Stock brought back Rees in place of Burgess. Orient pounded away at Vale's defence doing everything but score. Then, after 18 minutes, Vale broke away and a miss-hit shot by Leake gave them a lucky lead. On one occasion near the end of the game Poulton hit a terrific 35 yard shot from the wing, but it was just tipped over the bar. So it was that Vale went into the semi-final. Orient were out, but were distinctly unlucky, as every fan will tell you. The team went on to concentrate on improving their League position, finishing eleventh. Pacey had a fine season, scoring 21 goals.

The 54/5 team was said to be the best Orient had ever had. The final placing certainly bears this out. There were some class new players such as Phil McKnight, Johnny Hartburn and possibly the best capture, Vic Groves. There was enough talent to give the opposition headaches and that is what they did. They began with a couple of good victories and won four out of five matches in October. They were now lying joint fourth from top and went from strength to strength.

On 6th November the team went to Exeter and made a devastating triumph. They went into the lead before the supporters had settled in with a goal after 35 seconds from Stan Morgan. The visitors equalised through a dubious penalty. Orient then tore the whole Exeter team in shreds. Vic Groves put one home and then Stan Charlton scored from 30 yards (Stan was born in Exeter, and his father once played for the club). In the second half young Groves, now signed professional for us, was revelling in the heavy conditions, and netted

two more for his hat-trick. The team received a standing ovation from the crowd at the end, and there was a merry journey home for them and the supporters. The same day Phil White was cheered off the pitch after a fantastic display of skill in the reserve's 4-2 victory over Southend. When the Exeter result came over the tannoy, a neutral observer, who had been saying he couldn't understand Stock leaving young White out of the first team, just blushed and hurried out of the ground. (I think he was a Spurs supporter). To add to this the Juniors knocked the Arsenal youth team out of the FA Youth Cup 3-1 at Highbury.

The first team were now second in the League, behind Bristol City, and had scored 31 goals in only eighteen games. 16,061 saw them undo Southend's first team 5-1 (they could have had ten quite easily)—Rees 2, Facey, Morgan and Blizzard. Not to be outdone, the reserves beat Clacton 7-0 in the Essex Professional Cup. They placed a couple of youngsters in the side, including Albert Woodison from Ramsgate, making a great debut with a hat-trick. Simmons scored two, and Sheckles and Burgess one each. The first team then won at Aldershot and went top of the League on goal average.

ANOTHER SEVEN

After this record win at Exeter, nobody expected a repeat. But very soon the same team, except for Hartburn, replacing Poulton, travelled to Torquay. This time Billy Rees started the slaughter. He got the ball from the opposing centre half and smashed in a great shot past the bewildered Torquay goalie, Jeffries. Little did he know what was to hit him later. In fact, only nine minutes after, Johnny Hartburn put the Orient two up with a header from a Ken Facey centre and five minutes later Facey himself scored when he saw their keeper out of his area and calmly lobbed the ball over his head and into the net. After Vic Groves put home a fourth, Torquay, unlike

Exeter previously, fought back and scored twice from Norman and Collins (a penalty). But Groves came up and headed in Orient's fifth from Hartburn's corner kick, and then scored again to complete a hat-trick. Finally Facey put in number seven. This grand result brought Orient's tally in the League up to 46 goals from 22 matches. Ken Facey was on 15, Groves 9 and Rees 7.

FRONT PAGE NEWS

That was the headline. After a draw at Northampton, the club programme announced that for the first time in our stormy history both teams were top of their respective Leagues. To celebrate, the first team hit Shrewsbury for five, Johnny Hartburn scoring an amazing hat-trick in only 3.5 minutes —the fastest ever scored by an Orient player, and one of the fastest in the League. On-form Vic Groves had a hand in all three. Shrewsbury had been punished by the slick, go-ahead methods of Orient's machine-like tactics. But soon the team started to slide, only picking up four points out of a possible eight, letting Bristol City go top. In one game Notts County came down to Brisbane Road and defeated us 2-1—a character named Tommy Johnston had much to do with that. A bigger setback was Vic Groves' injury in the game at Swindon, after which they could only hold the relegation threatened club to a 0-0 draw. We were in another sticky patch. Once again the supporters rose to the occasion with their chant:

Up the O's. I can 'ear yer.
Up the O's, is our slogan.
We take the reverses with a smile.
Are we downhearted? Never!

And just before Easter the team slammed Torquay at home, 5-0. Big Stan Morgan bagged four (it was on boat race day), thus giving us our best ever double. Bristol were still in tremendous form and so the table at this stage was like this:

Vic Groves

	P	W	D	L	F	A	P
1st Bristol City	39	26	6	7	88	42	59
2nd ORIENT	37	23	6	8	78	32	54
3rd Southampton	38	22	8	8	63	39	52

So it was all to play for after Easter and they did well to finish runners-up. Unfortunately, at this time, only one team was promoted. In scoring 41 goals away from home they passed their previous best, 36, back in 31/2. And in winning ten away games they bettered their 24/5 total. The reserves had a great season too, ending fifth in division 2 of the Combinations. Fans will tell you they were one of the best and most entertaining sides we ever had, and people as good as Phil White and Fred Fisher deserved more than a couple of first team outings. In the FA Cup the first team beat Western League Frome Town 3-0 away, but fell 1-0 to Workington at home.

PROMOTION AT FIFTY

Alec Stock brought some fresh faces to Brisbane Road during the close season: experienced back Jack Gregory came from Southampton; Ronnie Heckman from Bromley and Len Julians, a forward from Walthamstow Avenue, both signed professional forms. Big centre half Lou Brahan, also from Walthamstow Avenue, joined as an amateur, and there was Jimmy Smith, a clever winger who could run and run, right through any game. How long could Orient keep Groves? Not long, many were saying. The club's board of directors said they needed £10,000 by October 15th or they would be forced to sell star players. It was announced in the club's programme for the Bournemouth match on 22nd September that the supporters club committee and others were to make an all-out attempt to collect the money. An appeal fund was set up. On the field the team were doing quite well, lying in fourth position, but then came a heavy defeat at Newport County, 3-0. The man to blame was Newport's Tommy Johnston, who scored a fantastic hat-trick; we had no answer.

Man in the news Vic Groves was in terrific form, and was now picked for the England B v Yugoslavia B game at Bristol. The national papers were spreading rumours about his relations with the club, but Groves told chairman Harry Zussman he wanted to stay, and that was the end of that. Then one evening, supporters read in their late edition that Stock had sold not only Groves, but popular Stan Charlton as well. Arsenal paid £30,000 for them, the money to be ploughed back into the club. Why did Groves change his mind? Apparently he had been tormented by all the publicity, worried that Arsenal would be expecting him to play like a second Stanley Matthews. When that had died down, constantly renewed offers had persuaded him. Billy Rees also went, to Headington (now Oxford United)—not that the team seemed to suffer.

They walloped Palace 8-0, a new record at Leyton Stadium. The gate, however, dropped to 10,000.

It was a fact that many fans went down to Highbury to watch their former heroes. But they missed a cracker of a match, and O's were now top of the table on goal average. What followed was quite remarkable. The forwards hit 7-4-4-4-4 in the League and Cup, not bad for a team that had just lost two of its stars. The forward line that appeared in these six high scoring games were: White, Facey, Burgess, Heckman and Hartburn. In the next match they beat Lovells Athletic in the first round of the Cup, a real feast of attacking soccer, one could only feel sorry for the Southern League side. The match was a personal triumph for Ronnie Heckman. He smashed in five (no other player in the history of the club has ever scored five in a League or Cup match). Even so, the man of this Cup-tie was Phil White. He was described by Lovell's manager as another Stanley Matthews. They hit fifteen goals in two matches. They entertained Brentford in the second round of the FA Cup and won convincingly again, scoring four goals and one supporter shouted out as the players left the field, 'Four for ever more'. Walsall were the next visitors to Brisbane Road, a visit they weren't really looking forward to after reading about Orient's scoring habits. And as soon as the whistle went they certainly knew what had hit them. In the opening twenty minutes they had no answer to our attacking power with Heckman, Facey, Hartburn and Burgess once more among the goals.

ON THE EDGES OF OUR SEATS

For the next match at Exeter City, Ken Facey had to drop out because of a heavy cold, so young Phil Woosnam came in. It ended 1-1 and Orient followed up with two more 2-2 draws, home and away against Norwich. They were still one point clear

Ken Facey, made over 300 League appearances for Orient in 10 years ▶

Johnny Pattison, forward

at the top of the table, and on 31st December the team came up with another convincing victory at home over Southend United. This was a good test to get the team in the right frame of mind for their third round Cup-tie against Plymouth Argyle, who were lying second from bottom in the second division. Everyone was looking to see just how good Orient really were, because if they wanted to go up they ought to beat teams like Plymouth. One goal turned out to be enough, scored by Johnny Hartburn after good work by Phil Woosnam. But in the League the team had fallen to third position, on 37 points, the same as Brighton and 3 behind Ipswich, though we had two games in hand. And so to 28th January, the day we faced Birmingham City in the Cup fourth round at Brisbane Road. Everyone remembered the fine victory at St.

Andrews in 52 when we won 1-0. Birmingham had, no doubt, planned to try to avenge that defeat. Alec Stock decided that the Orient should change their colours for this important game to the famous white shirts with the red V, a great decision for every O's fan. It was guaranteed that the fans would cheer the team throughout the game because of those old shirts and all the mystique that went with them. But on the day the team were well beaten 3-0.

STOCK RESIGNS

Suddenly it was announced that Alec Stock had resigned, to take over at Arsenal. A bolt from the blue for the supporters, and this is how the manager explained it in the programme.

"I thought it only right in view of my recent resignation that I should write for the first time in this programme, the first time in the seven seasons that I have been here.

My resignation was a decision that was not taken lightly as it had been under consideration for three months. It was not to be hurried as my position as manager with the Orient was unique, as far as modern football goes. During my stay at Orient, I have been treated with every respect and consideration by all, from the president of the club, chairman and directors, staff and players, officers and members of the supporters club and spectators. It is recognised in football circles that the Orient, from within, is the happiest of all clubs and this I can only illustrate by stating that in the seven seasons I have been here (through thick and thin) no director has ever asked me, 'What is the team for Saturday?' This does not mean they are disinterested, but only tends to show the degree of liberty I have enjoyed here.

In this respect I would most sincerely like to place on record my appreciation of the delightfully happy and contented time I have had with the club. Much of the joy of being connected with the Orient springs from the chairman, Mr. Harry Zussman, and to him for his friendship and advice I shall be ever grateful. To the other members of the board I also offer a thousand thanks.

This handsome treatment has also been the lot of the members of the staff and players, and I can assure you that it has been reflected in the results the club has achieved and certainly over the past three seasons. Another abiding memory of Leyton Orient is the unique position of the supporters club. It is in my opinion the best is existence.

No manager can be successful without the goodwill of players, and in this I have been very lucky. I sincerely trust

Billy Rees, a great forward in the 50's

that they have derived as much pleasure and fun as I have over the last few seasons. In handing over the reins to my personal friend, Les Gore, I wish him and everyone connected with the club continued success, good health and good luck. Some criticism can be levelled at the timing of my leaving the Orient in relation to the club's promotion prospects, but knowing the strength of the staff and the ability and loyalty of the players I have no doubt that Orient will continue the good work from where I left off. Up the O's."

How would this upheaval effect the team's play? A goal by Hartburn clinched 1-0 a very tight match with Reading, and as all the lads trooped off the pitch they heard the great news that Ipswich Town were beaten by Crystal Palace at home 1-0, which brought us to within a point of them with two games in hand.

TOMMY JOINS UP

At home to Newport County, who beat us earlier in the season with 3 goals from Tommy Johnston, revenge was sweet. Julians 2, and White, made it 3-1 in our favour. But the other one, Newport's 1 was yet again the work of Scotsman Johnston. After it was over some of our players, in particular Stan Aldous, suggested to Les Gore and Harry Zussman that they sign Johnston on. In the end they did persuade him, and they paid £6000 plus Mike Burgess, (the supporters club gave £1000 of this). Johnston had scored 22 goals so far that season for Newport, and he soon became a firm favourite with the O's fans.

The League table was looking exciting. We were on top with 51 points, two points ahead of Ipswich and two games in hand. Two more victories and Orient were now 3 points clear. Many fans were already celebrating, but it wasn't over yet. At Easter they won 3-2 at home to Torquay and the following day 25,000 fans saw the top of the table clash against Brighton. We lost 1-0, and this meant that they had to go back to Torquay and this time win, if we weren't to be toppled. Injuries forced changes. In came Sid Bishop, Jimmy Smith and Len Julians, and it was Julians who once again was there at the right time. He scored twice and Heckman once in a fine 3-1 victory.

STOCK RETURNS

During the week there came sensational news. Alec Stock had changed his mind. He was giving up at Arsenal (after only 53 days away). Brisbane Road welcomed him back with a capital W, and he wrote in the club magazine: "Hard as I tried I could never stop thinking about Orient. My mind said Arsenal, my heart said the O's.....I realised the friendship to me was much more important, much more valuable than all the progress and prestige I may have achieved at Highbury..." As manager, he took the team down to Southampton—another fine fight with Orient remaining masters. Len Julians scoring twice and many thousands of O's supporters amongst the 18,699 crowd. Len, who patiently awaited a comeback to the League side, never let the side down once when he rejoined. He scored 10 goals as well as 18 for the reserves. The team beat Shrewsbury 5-2 at home. Just before half-time Tommy Johnston scored the fourth, Orient's 100th League goal of the season, the very first time an Orient team had scored this many in a season. The position looked like this:

	P	W	D	L	F	A	P
1st ORIENT	41	28	8	5	102	36	64
2nd Brighton	43	27	7	9	104	46	61
3rd Ipswich Town	42	22	13	7	99	57	57

We were almost there, but lost 2-0 at home to Ipswich Town, to keep all the club's followers on thorns. And so to Thursday 26th April 56 and a match versus Millwall. 22,344 came to cheer O's on to, they hoped, division 2. The first half was goalless, but in the second Hartburn swung over a corner and somehow the ball curled into the net. Then, to the dismay of the Orient crowd, Johnny Scummers scored. What a relief it was when Tommy Johnston drove the ball into the roof of the net after shots from White, Facey and Woosnam had been cleared off the line. Millwall still fought hard because they were in dire trouble in the League, second from bottom. But the champagne flowed with the tears. The older fans had waited a long time for this moment. In Orient's jubilee year, it was good to see many old faces at the game. Arthur Banner, Vic Groves and Stan Charlton, amongst others, cheered the O's on to victory. The division three championship (south) shield was presented to happy club chairman Harry Zussman at the last game by the League's president, Mr. Arthur Oakley J.P., (the way the O's had been shooting on target all

The record scoring Tom Johnston ▶

season, Annie Oakley should have been there too). Stanley Rous also attended, and watched as the players and officials paraded the shield around the pitch. The final positions were these:

	P	W	D	L	F	A	P
1st ORIENT	46	29	8	9	106	49	66
2nd Brighton	46	29	7	10	112	50	65
3rd Ipswich Town	46	25	14	7	106	60	64

Fair haired Ron Heckman scored 29 League and Cup goals, which was a new Orient record, with Cup goals included. Frank Neary's League record of 26 goals in 48/9 stayed. But still, Heckman's total of 23 equalled Ted Crawford's effort in 35/6. Les Gore, when he took over as manager had a fantastic spell; the results read: played 10, won 9, lost 1, goals for 30, against 11, points 18. What a record, plus the fact that Gore signed Tommy Johnston, a player who must have been the bargain of the year. Johnny Hartburn, not to be out-done, created a new record of goals scored from the wing, 20 League and 3 Cup. It was also a wonderful season off the field: the club made a profit of £17,965 (another record), and plans were put forward for a new stand. At the close there was the tragic news that John 'Taffy' Evans had died, at the age of only 31. He did a lot of work on the field to make promotion possible, and was one who lifted Orient from the depths in 51-2-3.

The stage was set. The new grandstand was completed by October and included new offices, medical room and many other fac-ilities. For the new season in the second division Alec Stock signed the following players: Stan Williams from Chelsea, Alex Forbes the former Scotland international from Arsenal, Jimmy Andrews and Dave Sexton from West Ham United, and Peter Carey was signed from Barking on amateur forms. The first match was at home to Nottingham Forest, the O's losing 4-1. There was a scare in that match when a small fire started in the new stand caused when a lighted cigarette was thrown on the floor,

but it was quickly put out. As chairman Harry Zussman joked: 'For years we hoped the old stand would catch fire to collect the insurance, and now the new one nearly goes up on its first day in use.'

The team made a steady improvement. Against Doncaster Rovers, Tommy Johnston was sent off. The club said they would appeal against the referee's decision. With the stand now completed and open they entertained West Ham in the League on 6th October. In the Hammers team were such well known faces as Malcolm Mus-grove, Malcolm Allison, John Smith. A crowd of 24,613 turned up and saw us lose 2-1. Stan Williams put the ball into his own net. Orient's luck was dead out in that game—borne out by a remark after the match of Reg Pratt, West Ham's chairman who, on receiving the glowing congratulat-ions and warm handshake of Harry Zussman, confessed,. 'Thank you, Harry, we were lucky. But we can do with the points.' Manager Stock declared 'It is up to us to make the ball run for us.' The findings of an FA disciplinary committee decided to take no further action in the case of Tommy Johnston. That cheered everybody up. On 10th October at Upton Park they played Southend United in the final of the Essex Professional Cup, and ran out winners with a goal from Heckman. This was the first time they had won the cup since its inauguration in 49. They had appeared in two finals before, both against Southend. This result seemed to buck the team up. At Blackburn they found themselves 3-1 down, but pulled back to level the scores. After twelve games the team were lying four off the bottom with only 19 points.

During the next few months they slowly but surely moved up the table. They went to Sheffield United, and as Manager Stock stated, it was the team's best win, and United's first defeat at home of the season. Again proving Orient's grand fighting qual-ities. It was good to see the old form of Ronnie Heckman and Tommy getting amongst the goals again. The team were now going from strength to strength. At home to Barnsley, Johnston scored two great goals; the visitors had no-one to match his finishing power. Even so, the Press were calling the O's the season's biggest flops. But we showed them, winning at Port Vale and then picking up 9 out of a possible 10 points. The team kept this great form up by beating Rotherham United 2-1 and Lincoln City 2-0 away. On the 15th December they went to Nottingham, and Tommy Johnston scored two beauties that put the team on the victory trail. They were now eighth from the top in the table, a fine performance after such a poor start. At Christmas they played Liverpool home and away. At Anfield in a close game, Liverpool won 1-0, roared on by 22,001 fans. Dave Groombridge made one of his fearless dives, this time at the feet of Billy Liddell, saving a certain goal. But he fractured his collarbone and had to be replaced by Phil McKnight, who had a fine game. In the return we lost 4-0. Orient had a break from the League with an all ticket home match against Chelsea in the Cup third round. They were unlucky in that match, well worth a score. They pounded at the Chelsea goal for most of the match; on one occasion Johnston went close with a header, and a blistering drive from little winger Smith, playing against his old club, struck the crossbar. Despite all the pressure Chelsea broke away and scored two goals, having all the luck.

The next League game was at home to second division from top Stoke City, which ended 2-2, (Johnston getting our two). They had a magnificent victory at Middlesborough, a brilliant team performance. It wasn't such a good start though, Brian Clough had the ball in the O's net inside 90 seconds. Our next match was at Upton Park for the local Derby. Many thousands of O's supporters boosted the crowd to 36,500. The Hammers got off to a flying start and eventually won 2-1. Blackburn Rovers were lying fourth from the top of the division and pushing hard for promotion, when we held them at home to a 1-1 draw, Ken Facey scoring. Nothing very much happened in the run-in to the end of the season, and we were quite safe in the table. The season finished with a home match against Notts County, 2-2 with goals from Andrews and Tommy Johnston—his 27th of the 56/7 season, breaking Frank Neary's record 26 in 48/9 season. All in all it was a good year for the team. They won eight of their away games, one more than they won at home. And O's were spoken of as promotion outsiders. The reserves also had a fine season; they finished third out of 32 teams in the big Combination League, scoring 115 goals and conceding 71. Len Julians had an outstanding season, breaking the reserve scoring record with 45 goals; this beat Tommy Foster's 34 scored in the 34/5 season. Len was unlucky in having to be Tom Johnston's deputy. Fans received a shock in the summer of 57 with the news that Alec Stock was leaving the Orient to take up the vacant manager's job at Roma FC in Italy. So once again Les Gore took over. The appointment of George Hicks as secretary was announced. The team got off to a terrible start—played three and lost three. They lost at Grimsby Town 7-2 on 24th August. But before October things were really looking up. They beat division leaders Charlton Athletic 3-2. Tom Johnston gave Orient the lead with a grand shot but from the restart Billy Kiernan levelled the score, the ball was in the back of the net before the defence realised. After five minutes, Johnston was on hand to drive home a ball which had only partially been saved by Duff from a shot by Sexton. Ronnie Heckman put us 3-1 up with a powerful free kick. Ayre got a second for Charlton and despite all their pressure the O's held out to win 3-2. Other great wins followed: over Cardiff City 4-2, over Middlesborough 4-0, with Julians cracking home four great goals. A 2-1 victory over Barnsley; and a fine 5-1 win over

Swansea Town. The team then went through a sticky patch of three defeats in a row. Les Gore decided to sell Ronnie Heckman to Millwall, with the team lying fifth from bottom on 14 points from eighteen matches. At this time Mark Lazarus signed professional forms for the club after playing as an amateur. He joined from Barking, and just 18 years of age, played his first game as a pro for the reserves against Southend United reserved on the 30th November. Lazarus showed his worth by scoring a great goal to level the match at 1-1. The first team drew at home to Notts County 2-2, followed by an exciting match at Ipswich Town, where we were beaten 5-3. The lads just couldn't get the breaks, though they beat Blackburn Rovers at home 5-1, with goals from Johnston 2, Julians 2, and White. This started a great revival of the team's performance over the next couple of months.

Tom Johnston's personal tally for the season was now 23, easily the leading goal-scorer in the Football League. Then came Grimsby Town to Brisbane Road, and we gained a sweet revenge for their beating us on the first day of the season 7-2, Johnston bringing his total so far to 26 with a great hat-trick followed with goals from Julians and Hartburn. They thrashed Rotherham United on Christmas Day, and what a present the team and especially Tom Johnston gave the 13,956, for he broke Orient's seasonal scoring record with 30 goals, beating Ronnie Heckman's 29 League and Cup effort in the 55/6 season and also breaking his own record of 27 last term. Then the team were off to Stoke. Facey came in for McKnight but City went into the lead in the seventh minute when winger Coleman gave Frank George no chance with a great shot. Orient began to come forward, and Johnston put in a bullet header, keeping up the pressure Julians scored a second just before half-time. The teams came out with the floodlights on and then Johnston nearly scored a third. He rounded the goalkeeper skilfully and was on his way to walking the

ball when up popped a Stoke defender to clear it off his boot, but only to Phil White on the byeline, and he made for goal and shot cleverly into the net, only for the referee to rule Johnston offside. They were so much on top that they simply had to score again and they did. Woosnam strode past the Stoke defence to score with a rasping shot. People around the club were talking of Johnston beating Dixie Dean's record of 60 goals in the 27/8 season. Dean was a master of scoring with his head, as was Johnston. The record for the second division was held by George Camsell of Middlesborough —59 goals from 37 matches. Johnston had already had three match balls presented to him for his two hat-tricks. The third Tommy gave to Phil White for helping him to that four with his great crosses.

The cup was here once again, starting at home to Reading in the third round and winning 1-0. After drawing 1-1 at Cardiff City on 18th January the team had to travel there the following week for the fourth round of the Cup and under Les Gore's instructions, reverted back to the old Clapton Orient's shirts, white with a red V, but the change didn't seem to bring much luck and they lost 4-1. In the League they beat Liverpool 1-0. It was good entertainment, Orient's goal coming from a penalty. Tom Johnston scored later with a fantastic 18 yard header, but Arthur Ellis ruled him offside. These two points put us in a safe position in the table. We were beaten 4-1 by West Ham at home; 25,000 admired the Hammers' fast attacking soccer.

JOHNSTON LEAVES, STOCK RETURNS

All Orient felt the shock when they heard that Tommy Johnston was leaving to join promotion chasing Blackburn Rovers for £15,000, many supporters were disgusted. The true story was as follows. It was true that Johnston wanted to leave and the club did not want to let him go. The big Scot felt he might be of some service to promotion contenders Blackburn. All that week Johnston had been chasing acting manager Les Gore. There was a board meeting where they tried to persuade him to stay, but Johnston was adamant and so, reluctantly they gave way, Johnston opened up negotiations with Blackburn manager Johnny Carey and he went up to Blackburn to complete the deal. Les Gore said: 'What's the use of keeping a disgruntled player, it hasn't been and never will be an Orient policy.' Johnston had scored 35 League, and 1 Cup goal that season. The supporters club held a farewell get-together for Tommy during which they gave him a tankard. Tom thanked the supporters club, officials and members for their gift which, he said, would find a place on his sideboard and serve always to remind him of his very happy association with Leyton Orient and all connected with it. The transfer was Les Gore's last duty as manager because Alec Stock was returning to Orient from Italy. Stock couldn't find a regular centre forward having tried quite a few after the departure of Johnston, (who was successful; his dream of first division football came true. Blackburn were promoted with Johnston scoring many vital goals). The team finished in twelfth position on 42 points.

Orient players McKnight and Woosnam were picked for the London team in the inter-League fairs match against Lausanne. During the season quite a few players showed promise, like Sid Bishop and Alan Eagles, though Stan Williams seemed to slow up and Stan Aldous' days as a first teamer were over. Cyril Lea was another newcomer who showed potential. Alec Stock made a few changes for the start of the new season. Joe Elwood for one; he had a couple of matches with the youth team at the end of last season. Promising youngster Malcolm Lucas came from Bradley Rangers. Stan Aldous joined Oxford United as a coach; he had made 302 appearances for our first team. Although they lost the first two games, there followed a run of victories over, among others, Derby, Ipswich and Barnsley. At Swansea Town's Vetch Field the game was overshadowed by a disputed goal, scored 25 minutes from the end, to put Swansea 3-2 ahead. Ivor Allchurch crossed the ball when it was several inches over the goal line, and Palmer hit it into the net. When the referee awarded the goal, the Orient players were dumbfounded, but despite protests, the goal stood. In the *Daily Mail* Peter Moss wrote: "Palmer's goal a disgrace: I did want to write the story of Des Palmer, Swansea's brave centre forward who came back after a long injury to score two goals. But the way his second goal came takes away all the gilt. It was a disgrace to the game."

In the *Daily Express* Jim Hill wrote: "Robbery. The Ref. ignores Orient: No-one will convince Leyton Orient, or me, that 3-3 was a true result last night. I say Orient won 3-2. Mark Lazarus made a fine League debut."

It was just as well that only five minutes later Phil McKnight scored the equaliser. Paddy Hasty had a great first game, scoring two fine goals. They beat Scunthorpe at home 2-1, cheered on by 15,955. Orient were now lying in fifth position on 10 points. They held a testimonial for Jimmy Smith, forced to quit the game because of an injury he received last session against Fulham. Famous names turned out for Jim, like Tom Johnston, Vic Groves, Bryan Douglas, Ron Springett, Jimmy Dickinson and Eddie Bailey.

WOOSNAM CAPPED FOR WALES

With the Orient home to Sheffield United, Phil Woosnam for Wales against Scotland at Cardiff, following such great Welshmen who appeared for Wales whilst with the O's as Lawrence, Mills and Morley. Woosnam had a great game. The Orient drew 1-1, Andrews scoring the goal. Stock gave O's supporters another shock when he sold Phil Woosnam to West Ham for £30,000. Many fans said it was a racket, but once again, as with Johnston, Woosnam wanted first division football and the club just couldn't stand in his way. Soon after the manager and directors went to Birmingham to watch old favourite Tommy Johnston playing for Blackburn Rovers. He was apparently a bit unsettled with them. Middlesborough came to Brisbane Road. Malcolm Lucas made his League debut and Mark Lazarus was again causing havoc on the wing. Julians scored a great hat-trick against Bristol City at home and Joe Elwood had the match of his life. He cracked in all Orient's four goals in their 4-2 win, a great effort.

At Christmas, Stock exchanged Len Julians for the former O's player Stan Charlton, a popular move from the fans' point of view. He also signed Arsenal's reserve centre forward Tony Biggs a couple of days later, and then experienced Eddie Baily, the big hearted cheeky chappie, who at first turned down the move. These signings must have been unique in the club's history, three players in the space of five days, which is some going, or rather, coming. Len Julians was another who wanted first division football; he jumped at the chance of joining the Arsenal. For us he made 67 League appearances and scored 35 goals, a good player. In a reserve game at Brisbane Road on the 17th January one man stood out, it was Eddie Brown, a real character. He was an authority on Shakespeare, also a male model. He would crack jokes with the crowd and was known to have shaken hands at the corner flags many a time. He showed his speed when scoring twice against our reserves in their 6-1 defeat. He impressed so much that Stock decided to bid for the experienced forward and within a couple of hours Bomber Brown was an Orient player—he was nicknamed Bomber because of his speed. His first game was in a friendly with QPR at Brisbane Road. It was a real cracker with the O's winning 9-1 (yes 9), Eddie Brown scoring 3. All these recruits were urgently needed. The team were in dire trouble, third from bottom in 19 points.

TOMMY COMES HOME

To everyone's delight Tommy Johnston signed on again for O's. Late on the Friday night before the next away match at Fulham, the wires between Leyton and Blackburn began to hum. Tom travelled through the night and actually signed only a few hours before the kick-off. Even so we lost 5-2. Johnny Haynes was in great form. Our goals were scored by Baily and Andrews.

They lost to Liverpool at home 3-1, but were out of luck and as the *Daily Mirror* wrote of the game: 'Orient's Joe Elwood crosses the ball, beats goalkeeper Tommy Younger, Eddie Brown shoots. The ball hits a post, rolls along the goal line. Younger grabs it, no goal. Liverpool's Alan A'Court crosses the ball, beats goalkeeper Frank George. Fred Morris shoots. The ball hits a post, and curls in, goal. That was the main difference between the teams, luck.'

Stock then resigned, but before he went, bought Harry Nicholson from Accrington —the biggest keeper since Arthur Wood, 13½ stone and over 6 feet tall. The team found a bit of form to lift them out of trouble. They thrashed Sunderland 6-0, Eddie Brown hitting 4, the others coming from Johnston and White. They beat Charlton 6-1 at home, Joe Elwood scoring a hat-trick, (Brown, Baily and Facey). The last match at Barnsley ended the right way, 3-1, and ensured them the 17th place. Johnston and Brown, in their short spell at the club, made that extra difference to the team. They finished joint top scorers on 19 goals along with Joe Elwood who was honoured by being picked to play for the Irish FA XI v The Army at Windsor Park, Belfast.

For the 59/60 season acting manager Les Gore signed mainly young players, with the O's playing so smoothly towards the end of last season no major new signings were made. The season got under way well. The team went to Aston Villa, the current

League leaders and, weathering the opening five minutes they went on to delight the 38,000 crowd with some fine football. It was a bitter blow when after 67 minutes Villa took the lead. Ken Facey, trying to intercept a pass to Gerry Hitchens, fell over; the ball hit Facey but went to Hitchens 10 yards out, who steered it past the helpless Groombridge. If the ball hadn't hit Facey, Hitchens and a few other forwards would have been offside. The Villa manager Joe Mercer told Les Gore: 'If the game had been decided on points, the Orient would have won by 10-0... The Orient are the best footballing side to visit Villa Park this season.' Aston Villa chairman confirmed what his manager had said, in fact, he went so far as to say that Orient played better than many first division clubs who visited Villa Park last season. After such glowing reports, the team pulled in a few more thousand for the visit of Sunderland, 16,335 in all. But they didn't see the O's at their best, only managing a 1-1 draw, Joe Elwood scoring. Against Middlesborough the team played some of the best football ever seen at Brisbane Road. They beat the 'Boro 5-0 and this result moved the team right up the table. Middlesborough, with three internationals in their team, Clough and Holliday (England), and Fernie (Scotland), were unfortunate victims. The O's put on a scintillating display. The game marked the return of Phil White to the team and young Dennis Sorrell's first outing. Eddie Brown scored a hat-trick. Brian Clough was marked out of the game by the ever improving Sid Bishop. At Anfield, 34,321 saw Liverpool snatch the lead after 15 minutes. Orient didn't waste any time, for a minute later McDonald sent over a fine cross for Johnston to head home 1-1. Liverpool regained the lead a minute later, but back came Johnston, heading home another McDonald cross, 2-2. With some great passing all over the giant Anfield pitch, the O's regained the lead when McDonald, having a great match, sent over another fine cross which the Liver-

pool keeper could only push straight into the path of young Dennis Sorrell, and he shot through a bunch of players and in off a post. Sorrell seemed to jump 20 feet into the air in sheer jubilation. Five minutes after the interval Dave Hickson equalised for Liverpool and when it seemed the O's had at least earned a point, Liverpool scored their fourth when Groombridge parried an Alan A'Court corner to the feet of Morris, who stabbed the ball into the net off Stan Charlton's legs. Everyone said Orient were the best team to visit Anfield in many years and the team received a grand ovation from the home supporters. They got the ball into the Liverpool net 6 times, only for three to be ruled offside. Tommy Johnston put his name into the record books when he scored his 200th League goal at Liverpool.

They were now in sixth position, chasing Aston Villa at the top. A few games later, dropping points, they found themselves 5-1 down at Ipswich. They hit back but eventually lost 6-3 (Foster 2 and Elwood). Against Huddersfield Town, Dennis Sorrell found himself marking the famous Scottish international Denis Law. Law hardly touched the ball, and on a TV interview that evening stated that Sorrell, 18 years old, was easily the best defender that had ever marked him. The next match was at home to the new League leaders Aston Villa, and in bad weather 17,000 turned out to see a great game, ending in a goalless draw. In the crowd was England team manager Walter Winterbottom, and he was very much impressed with two players—young Ron Foster of the O's and Villa's Gerry Hitchens.

Cardiff City were leading the second division when they came to Brisbane Road. The best crowd of the season, 22,918, witnessed a fantastic match, the O's finally losing 4-3 with goals from Johnston (2) and McDonald. They weren't discouraged by the defeat and won 2-1 at Hull City, although a goal down after only four minutes, when Stan Charlton handled the ball and Gubbins scored from the spot. Near the end of the season the team beat Liverpool at Brisbane Road, revenge for the defeats at Anfield earlier in the season. They finished in tenth position. In mid March Joe Elwood was honoured by playing for Ireland B v France B. The reserves finished in a fine fifth position in their League, with Peter Burridge ending the leading scorer on 14, Joe Elwood on 9 and Mark Lazarus with 7.

The 60/1 season wasn't the best in the club's history and they had quite a struggle to avoid relegation. However, they escaped the drop when Tommy Johnston scored against his old club Norwich City on 22nd April 61. For the new season "call me what you like" Les Gore made four signings, and he let Peter Burridge go to Millwall. Mark Lazarus was placed on the transfer list at his own request because he couldn't get first team football. The second home game was quite an occasion, against Brighton on Wednesday 31st August 60. The new floodlights, installed during the summer for a cost of around £15,000 were on and Orient won 2-1. Bishop and Facey scored for us and Adrian Thorne for the seasiders. The first two or three months were a mixture of good wins and shoddy defeats. One good win was at Leeds, when Malcolm Graham returned to the side and made sure of the points when he ran on to a great pass from Tom Johnston and hit an unstoppable shot for the third goal, after Waites and Johnston had scored earlier, (17,500). But in the return a couple of weeks later Leeds won 1-0. By this time Orient were lying ninth from the top on 8 points, chasing Norwich and Ipswich Town with 11 each. Yet a few matches later the team were struggling, so Les Gore went to Chelsea and signed goalkeeper Bill Robertson. It was sad news when Dave Groombridge was forced to retire from the game at the age of 30. He made 133 League appearances. Mark Lazarus by this time had left the club and moved to QPR for a small fee. After a bad showing at Rotherham United, losing 2-1, the team faced a long trip to the potteries to play Stoke City, who were unbeaten at home so far. Things looked bad for the team when City went into an early lead, but half an hour later Johnston picked up the ball and slipped it through to Brown who cracked home a great 20 yard shot, for the equaliser. Soon after Brown won the ball, ran on to the wing, and sent over a perfect cross for Johnston to nod home. That proved to be the winner, and kept the team off the bottom of the table on only 10 points.

On the same day at Brisbane Road the O's blooded young Harry Gregory in the reserve team and he made a good start, scoring two goals in the team's 5-2 victory over Leicester City reserves. Manager Gore announced that he had tried to sign two forwards from Arsenal, Joe Haverty and Jimmy Bloomfield, but the Gunners didn't want to part. Orient's pitch was getting quite a lot of bad publicity, especially after a game with Lincoln City in which the match was played under the most terrible conditions, and in front of only 5,793. Brown scored for us but it wasn't enough, Lincoln won 2-1. This, and the torrential rain, caused many matches to be called off and the team suffered some heavy defeats, especially away from home. Liverpool 5-0 and Les Gore went out again and signed Derek Gibbs from Chelsea, wingers Errol Crossan from Norwich City and Ron Newman from Portsmouth. Next followed a match against Luton Town at Brisbane Road, and Orient found themselves one down at half-time. Sid Bishop came up field and hit a terrific equaliser and with only a couple of minutes left Sealey scored a cheeky goal when he backheaded the ball into the net in front of a delighted 11,918 crowd. Two very useful points in the fight against relegation.

During the week Gore was on the look-out for a new forward, before the transfer deadlines. He was in Birmingham watching a reserve match when he spotted Wally St. Pier, West Ham's chief scout. Gore asked him about Andy Smillie, the Hammers young forward. No chance, said St. Pier. Then he enquired about Dave Dunmore. The fee was £12,000, far too much for us. So Gore suggested a straight swop, Dunmore for Alan Sealey, and after many hours the deal finally went through. So, 27 year old Dunmore became an Orient player and young Sealey joined the Hammers after playing only four League games and scoring 1 goal. In his home debut against Huddersfield Town, Dave put over a great centre for Graham to head home, and in the second-half hit a fierce drive from fully 20 yards which caught the Huddersfield goalkeeper off balance and the ball dropped into the net. In the run-in the team picked up four points out of a possible eight, but those were good enough to keep us in division two. They won at home to Stoke City 3-1 in front of 8,349, with goals from Graham 2, and Tom Johnston—as mentioned the vital goal that made us finally safe. This was to be the last League goal Johnston ever scored for the club, and he got, as always, a great reception from the crowd. So we finished in a poor 19th position. In the Cup, Orient made some good ground. Round three saw them at third division Gillingham. They soon showed their superiority and were four goals up inside 20 minutes, and went on to win 6-2. The team then had to face the mighty Southampton who had knocked out Ipswich Town 7-1 (Ipswich at that time were leaders of the second division). What prospect for the O's at the Dell? Half way through Derek Gibbs picked up a pass from Joe Elwood and swung around to hit a shot from over 25 yards into the Saints' net. Soon after Gibbs hit another mighty shot from the same spot, only to see the ball strike the crossbar and come out. Orient were well on top and deserved their victory. In the fifth round they were at home to Sheffield Wednesday, and got off to a good start. Yet no matter how hard they tried, they couldn't get past England goalkeeper Ron Springett. Eventually Wednesday scored. They forced

the pace, and scored again when big centre forward Ellis bundled Frank George into the goal. Surprisingly the goal was given.

This season saw the start of the Football League Cup and Orient were drawn at Chester in the first round. They went into a two goal lead through Foster and Brown, but Chester fought back and scored two fine goals to force a replay. This was to be Eddie Brown's last season at the Orient. He confessed that these times were among his happiest. No Orient fan will forget Bomber Brown's antics on the field, he livened up many a dull game. He would often sit on the wall surrounding the pitch and have a chat with the crowd, and must have been one of the fastest movers we ever had. He made 63 appearances, scoring 28 League goals for us and achieved a fine record of 200 League goals in the match for Orient versus Bristol Rovers. The club announced that it was their first priority to get the pitch in good condition again. The start of the 61/2 season saw the appointment of Johnny Carey as manager of the club; Les Gore reverting to his first love, number one trainer. Carey as a player won 40 international caps and never lost his place until his retirement from football in 53. During this period he had been a Manchester United player. In 53 he was appointed manager of Blackburn Rovers and he won them promotion in 58. A few months later he joined Everton as manager and in two years he bought and sold players worth £2.5m. In the summer of 61 he joined Leyton Orient FC as manager.

He soon caused a sensation by leaving out Tommy Johnston from the side. It was Carey who bought Johnston from the Orient when Blackburn Rovers paid £15,000 for him in 58. Maybe Carey thought that at the age of 34 Johnston was past his best. What a grand record Tom had for the club. He made 181 appearances in two spells at the Orient, scoring 121 League and 2 Cup goals. He still holds the club's seasonal scoring record of 36 goals in the 57/8 season, and he was top Football League scorer with 43 that season, whilst with the O's and Blackburn, (at no other time have we had the League's top goalscorer at the actual time he topped the list). It was a shame he had to miss one of the best seasons in the club's history, for he was later transferred to Gillingham for about £3,000, where he played mainly mid-field.

THEIR FINEST HOUR

Orient opened at Newcastle United, newly relegated, and drew 0-0, which surprised many fans. The first home match was against Southampton, who won 3-1. The home match against Middlesborough saw a drop of over 3,000 fans. Walsall were unbeaten at home for over 16 months. But in the inhuman heat of over 80 degrees, Orient beat them 5-1 with some fine push and run football, under the influence of Eddie Baily the club coach, and Foster after only five minutes put us on the victory trail. Dunmore, in the 44th minute, made it 2-0, then Graham came into the act and scored a hat-trick. Against Derby at home, the crowd came back. 12,316 watched Dave Dunmore race down the wing and hit a low drive goalwards. The ball hit Swallow and went straight into the net. In the second half Terry McDonald saw a good effort punched off the line by a defender. Dunmore shot home the penalty. This was the team's fourth consecutive win. They continued their fine form with a victory away at Stockport County in the first round of the FL Cup, 1-0, the goal coming from McDonald. They faltered during their next few matches gaining only one point out of six. But once they found their form, they hit three goals past Stoke City in the first 45 minutes. Many of the 10,621 crowd thought they were in for a goalscoring treat, but no more goals came in the second half. In the League Cup the O's hoped to do the same to first division Blackpool, and the famous Stanley Matthews; but they couldn't quite manage

Johnny Carey, manager

it, drawing 1-1 with a goal from Gibbs. In the replay at Blackpool we were hit 5-1.

In what was thought would be a tough promotion battle at Sunderland, Dave Dunmore gave us the lead after only 10 minutes with a header from a Foster centre. But it was Brian Clough who beat the O's. Firstly he beautifully controlled a high ball and hit it past the stunned Frank George, who got his hands to the ball but could only help it into the net. Then in the 52nd minute, Clough tried his luck with a hard low drive. The ball flashed into the net past George and it proved to be the winner. Things didn't look too good for us, with the prospect of a visit to top of the League

Liverpool. Yet the team put up one of its best displays for many a season, drawing 3-3, the Kop were in full cry for both teams. We learned later that Lucas was watched by Welsh selectors. 13,120 came to see the Derby match against Charlton Athletic. It was big Dave Dunmore who won the game for Orient with one of his specials, and a penalty. The O's found some good form, winning eight games on the trot. They won a grand match away at Middlesborough 3-2, with goals from Foster 2, and Dunmore, and were now only a point behind Liverpool, the leaders. Playing Swansea Town at Leyton Stadium it was Dunmore again who settled it. The ball came over; big Dave controlled it with his knee, and cracked it into the net. At this time, the Orient club supporters presented a plaque to Malcolm Lucas in honour of his recognition by the Welsh international selectors, plus the fact that he was made captain. Funnily enough, the lads had to travel to Wales to face Swansea again over Easter. Dynamo Dunmore hit a terrific hat-trick to finish any hope for the Welsh, O's winning 3-1.

They had a break from the League with a visit to Brentford in the third round of the Cup, drawing 1-1. In the replay at Leyton Stadium the better footballing side won. Although the Bees put up a great fight, Orient came through with goals from Foster and Elwood, watched by a truly appreciative audience of 26,690. In the next round they drew with Burnley. In the replay Orient almost ran their visitors off the park. But Adam Blacklaw made some great saves to keep us out and Burnley finally came through 1-0 with a lucky goal.

These Cup games seemed to upset the team for the vital League run-in. They lost three matches in a row, two at home. Norman Deeley from Wolves was then signed for £12,500, and young Gordon Bolland for £9,000. Little Deeley scored from a corner in his home debut against Sutherland. The ball seemed to drift goalwards and into the net, making it 1-1 and a much needed point against the nearest promotion challengers. Carey then sold Dennis Sorrell to Chelsea. Many thousands of fans travelled to Charlton to swell the 30,000 crowd, their heroes taking an early lead when, after good work by McDonald, Deeley scored with a fine shot. Dave Dunmore's thigh injury was giving him trouble, reducing his fire-power, and still Orient went forward. It paid off when Mal Graham hit a 25 yard cracker which poor Willy Duff could only fumble on its way. Charlton did hit back with a Kinsey header and went for an equaliser after the interval, but Orient held out for two more golden points.

FULL INTERNATIONAL CAP FOR LUCAS

Malcolm Lucas, the first player since Phil Woosnam in 58 to receive international honours, was now picked for the full Welsh national side, and played very well against Ireland. Over Easter they needed to win badly against Luton on the Monday, having failed to score in their last three matches, and they had to fight all the way to do it, 3-1. So it all depended on the last match at home to Bury. It was on 28th April 62. Liverpool had already clinched promotion and it was left to either Orient or Sunderland to follow them up. Sunderland had to travel to Swansea, who also had to win to avoid going down. Mal Graham came in as a very late substitute for the injured Ronnie Foster. The excitement at Brisbane Road was tremendous, and the teams came out amid deafening noise. Orient looked tense, though they started well on top and eventually scored with a great header from Graham. The sheds erupted. The referee blew his whistle for half-time—how were Sunderland doing? There were plenty of transistors tuned in to the Swansea v Sunderland broadcast. They were winning 1-0. Carey made sure the players were not told. When they came out again Bill Robertson made a tremendous save to keep us in the game.

1962. Players celebrate reaching div 1

All of a sudden the crowd erupted again. Swansea had equalised against Sunderland. Not too long to go. A few minutes later Malcolm Graham beat a Bury defender, raced into the penalty area, dribbled around the Bury goalkeeper, and drove low and hard into the empty net for his and Orient's second goal. Everybody went wild with delight, none more so than Chairman Harry Zussman. Graham in tears of joy, was mobbed by his team mates and young boys who ran on to the pitch. The final minutes were nerve racking. Eventually (it seemed like years) the referee blew his whistle. The pitch was invaded by thousands of fans, Graham was almost suffocated and captain Stan Charlton was chaired off the pitch. Chants of 'We want Carey' rang round the ground. Then over the air, came the news that Swansea had held Sunderland to a draw. The mighty O's were up. Carey, and those players who escaped the fans appeared in the directors box to give the crowd a wave. The champagne and players tears were flowing freely; they threw their shirts into the crowd. The pubs in the area were in for a busy night.

Manager Carey later said that the club owed a lot to coach Eddie Baily and trainer Les Gore and the defence must take fair

Malcolm Musgrove, an O's forward from 62-66 ▲
Welsh International Phil Woosnam ▼

credit for this fine season. Big Dave Dunmore finished top scorer with 22. Many sports writers stated that he should lead the England attack, but he was never chosen. The Dunmore of 61/2 season will go down as one of our best centre forwards. What an amazing season it had been for Leyton Orient Football Club. The first team had gained promotion into the first division for the very first time in the club's history. They also gave eventual runners-up Burnley a great fright in the FA Cup. The reserves won the Football Combination (Midweek Section). The young team won the Seanglian League Cup and were runners-up in their League. Among the players were Alan and Len Cheesewright, R. Deeks, I. Huttley and D. Clarke. Ken Facey captained the team in this, his last season with Orient. What a splendid player he turned out to be for us. He joined in 52 and made 301 appearances, scoring 74 League goals. He made many Cup appearances, scoring 5 goals, and must rank amongst Orient's best players. Everyone connected with the club deserved praise for this wonderful season, never forgetting the fans, whose loyalty gained some reward at last.

DIVISION 2, 1961/2

	P	W	D	L	F	A	P
Liverpool	42	27	8	7	99	43	62
ORIENT	42	22	10	10	69	40	54
Sunderland	42	22	9	11	85	50	53
Scunthorpe	42	21	7	14	86	71	49

THE FOOTBALL COMBINATION
MIDWEEK SECTION

	P	W	D	L	F	A	P
ORIENT	34	21	6	7	74	42	48
Portsmouth	34	20	6	8	72	47	46
Birmingham City	34	19	7	8	60	35	45

Crisis & Recovery

Carey as he had stated gave the team that took the club up the chance to prove themselves. In the close season the final wing of the grandstand was completed at considerable expense, and the terracing in the west stand was improved. On 18th August, they played Arsenal, who had big new signing Joe Baker from Torino in their team. They lost 2-1 and on the following Wednesday they lost again, to West Brom. Their very first point came at Birmingham where Graham and Dunmore levelled the game 2-2. Then they beat West Ham 2-0, and Hammers just couldn't get into the game even with the likes of Moore, Peters, Woosnam, Sealey and 'Budgie' Byrne. They had a good week, outplaying the great Manchester United—only the brilliance of keeper Dave Gaskell kept the score down to 1-0—Denis Law (also from Torino, costing £115,000), David Herd, Johnny Giles, Bill Foulkes and all. But this was nothing. On the Wednesday they put on one of their best performances ever to beat Everton at home 3-0 (Dunmore, Deeley, and young Bolland's first League goal). In the spell of defeats which followed, they lost the halfway place and then became fixed at the bottom of the table.

They were in trouble. Their lack of confidence showed at third from bottom Liverpool where, in front of TV cameras they were thrashed 5-0. During the week Malcolm Lucas picked up another full international cap against England at Wembley. Johnny Carey was a worried man and he made a few changes for the next home match against Wolves. They lost 4-0 and the fans slow handclapped. Was all this due to the club failing to buy players at the start of the season? After another defeat, at Arsenal 2-0, Carey went into the transfer market when, to everyone else, all seemed lost. He signed Malcolm Musgrove from West Ham for about £11,000 and the lad did well in the 2-2 draw with Birmingham. This was the winter of the big freeze-up which caused havoc with the League programme, and from mid December to February soccer came almost to a standstill. On 16th February they played Fulham, a crucial match since Fulham were one place above them in the table, but they lost 2-1.

There was a drop of over 4,000 in attendance for the home game against Manchester City. Carey made more changes: back came Mal Lucas, and Joe Elwood moved into the forward line. The match was drawn 1-1. At Blackpool on 2nd March they lost 3-2. With all these bad results the following statement was issued through the club programme to quash certain malicious rumours that had been floating about the football world:

You just can't stop bad rumours, and rumours have it that Orient are not making any sort of ground or attempt to strengthen the side to avoid relegation. What utter rubbish and nonsense. First and foremost the right sort and type of players are not easily found, and secondly the exorbitant size of transfer fees being demanded these days does not tend to ease the complications. Sad to say, and it is no secret, Orient are not in the happy position of being able to fork out indiscriminately large sums of money on new recruits. When a purchase is contemplated it has to be, as far as

O's v Portsmouth, 22.8.64. O's Gregory nearly scores

possible, well and wisely spent. For instance, a fee of £30,000 could be paid for a player only to find after all he does not fit into Orient's pattern of things, or that he is not a great deal better than the man he is supposed to replace in the team. Some clubs can afford to do this, and not miss it. It is not like that with Orient. Orient's management is fully aware of the weaknesses and the deficiences. It's as simple as that, but it is not so simple when hard cash has to be spent in the best way possible. The recent freeze-up badly hit the finances of many League clubs up and down the country. Orient is no exception. No matches means no gates, and that means no receipts. During the long spell some noble and magnificent sacrifices were made in this club, and those concerned should be warmly applauded and admired. Orient's board of directors do, and will, give manager Johnny Carey all the support they can, and believe me, he is an appreciative and patient man, always trying to do what is the best for Orient, so squash those rumours now.

The club tried to sign Jimmy McIlroy from Burnley at least three times. Carey did manage to sign Bobby Mason from Chelmsford for £15,000 and tall Scottish reserve forward Bob Grant. The team then lost five matches on the trot, one at White Hart Lane, losing 2-0 to Spurs watched by a crowd of over 40,000. They did win at Bolton 1-0, with a goal from Dave Dunmore, the team's first since 29th September, and followed up with a home draw against Blackburn Rovers 1-1. They lost their last four games of the season. The last match was away at Manchester United, who had to win to avoid going down with us. Things looked bad for them when Dunmore gave Orient the lead midway through the first half but United roared on by a crowd of 33,000, won 3-1 with a late burst of goals, Bobby Charlton scoring the third with a great shot—the final goal to be scored against us in division 1. Despite the lack of success in the League, the defence played well, Sid Bishop and Stan Charlton were particularly good. And they made some progress in the FA Cup. They were drawn at home to Hull City and won the replay, in round four they beat Derby at home very easily 3-0 (Dunmore, Deeley and Elwood). They wished all their matches in the League could have been like that. In the fifth round, against Leicester, they played their hearts out, but City, with Gordon Banks, Frank McClintock and Mike Stringfellow playing very well had the edge.

They reached the quarter-final of the League Cup. They forced a replay at Newcastle, which they took to extra time, and then Deeley and Graham scored. In the third round they were at home to Chester and really went to town, scoring nine goals to equal their 33/4 record. In the fourth round they played a great game at home to Charlton and won 3-2, but home again in the quarter-final to Bury they lost 2-0. The end of the club's very first season in the top division, and what a disaster it was. The side that were so magnificent in taking them there just couldn't sustain their heroic efforts. Many supporters publicly stated that the players who were sold during the season were better than the ones bought with the money. The only thing that cheered the fans up at the end was winning the Essex Professional Cup again, beating Colchester 4-2.

CAREY GOES

Johnny Carey had decided to leave the club before the 63/4 season began and manage Nottingham Forest. Quite a few well known players also left: Gibbs and Graham were transferred to QPR and three goalkeepers went on free transfers. The only signings were Gerry Ward from Arsenal, young keeper Peter Vasper, David Webb who played forward or defence, and goalie Reg Davies. They started very well indeed, building some really good form, putting new heart into the fans. They beat all types of teams, and even lost a few times, once to Portsmouth 6-3, and this match saw the return of Phil White, out through injury all last season—surely he would have excelled himself in the first division? Manager Gore didn't make any rash changes, only bringing in Mike Pinner for the injured Reg Davies, at Bury. The much improved Gordon Bolland clinched it with two good goals. After the game it was announced that Mr. Benny Fenton, currently manager of Colchester would take over officially as manager from 17th November. During the home match against Northampton, who seemed to play particularly hard, Gordon Bolland was knocked down quite a few times, which annoyed the 11,532 crowd to such an extent that a plastic-flighted dart was thrown on to the pitch. Once again the FA instructed Orient to place warning notices around the ground, and in the programme: if anything like that was done again the ground would be closed.

FENTON TAKES COMMAND

The new manager was a former player for Millwall, West Ham and Charlton, so he knew the London scene. Before his first game as manager, against Leeds at home, the 'Panthers' pop group entertained the crowd. The 'Soundcasters' also played from time to time after this. The game itself didn't please Fenton too much. As a whole they put up a fair display, but the forwards had their usual trouble in finding the net, and eventually Leeds got on top and scored with goals twice. With players like Giles, Hunter and Bremner they never looked like losing that lead. Fenton made a couple of changes for the next game, bringing back Deeley and Dunmore, and that worked, the team beating Rotherham away 4-2. However, the club were drifting dangerously near the bottom of the table. With the prospect of playing Leicester at Filbert Street in the third round of the FA Cup Fenton decided that the front line needed more punch; he brought in Harry Gregory and moved Dave Dunmore on to the wing. That was very intelligent; the players moved well in the new positions producing more moves that gave them a 2-1 victory.

The next tie was at home to West Ham. A record crowd turned out, 34,345. But the game was inconclusive and so it was over to Upton Park for the replay. The Hammers, in devastating form, scored three times in the first half and, although in the closing minutes Standen somehow kept out a fierce drive from Dunmore, the evening belonged to West Ham. In the League Cup they had already been beaten by West Ham 2-1. Back on League duty they beat Middlesborough 3-2 on 1st February. They then lost four matches on the trot. Only 4500 turned up to see Gordon Bolland score what was to be his last goal for Orient when they drew 2-2 against Scunthorpe; soon after he was transferred to Norwich for £30,000. Bolland, signed from Chelsea, had made 63 appearances and scored 19 goals. Benny Fenton signed Ted Phillips from Ipswich for £8,000. The team won 2-1 at Northampton and picked up four points out of six over the Easter period. They beat Swindon full backs Stan Charlton and Mike Hollow, playing very well against fast wingers Don Rogers and Mike Summerbee. They had to face Leeds away and Sunderland at home, both wanting points to gain promotion. At Leeds they played well but lost 2-1, and Sunderland gave them a pounding at Brisbane Road, their inter-national Johnny Crossan getting the third in their 5-2 victory.

On the 13th April at home to Cardiff City they put up a great display to win 4-0 and avoid relegation. Cardiff, who had the famous Charles brothers, Mel and John, as well as Ivor Allchurch, just couldn't get going. The club arranged a testimonial for Phil White on 31st April, and many former players turned up including Tommy Johnston, Phil Woosnam, Ron Heckman, Les Julians and Frank George. Phil had signed forms for us in 53, from Wealdstone, and despite many clubs chasing his signature he remained a one-club man. Tom Johnston would be the first to admit that 'Whitie' played a major role in assisting him to achieve the goalscoring record. Phil turned out 221 times for the team and scored 28 goals, but he made hundreds for others. In aid of the Leyton borough fete the lads played a game against the TV All Stars, and the scoreline read—wait for it— 11-11. Among others, Terry Downes, Bernard Bresslaw, Stan Stennett and Kenneth Cope, played. The final League placing was sixteenth on 36 points. The hopes that they would reach again for the first division were dashed.

DEEPER IN

During the summer of 64 Fenton made quite a few signings. The Orient youth team were doing very well, with such players as Terry Price, David Webb, Billy Carter, Peter Vasper, Barry Watling and Jimmy Scott. The first team started the new term with a bang, hitting Pompey 5-2, Phillips scoring a hat-trick. Phillips was very soon close to a total of 200 League goals, though the team were not doing all that well. Fenton went out and bought back Dennis Sorrell from Chelsea. Then he sold Malcolm Lucas to Norwich. The team lost 2-1 at Bury and with an away fixture at Swansea looming up things didn't look too bright. But youth was being given a chance, and a signing, a tall centre forward called Andy

O's Northampton, 17.10.64. O's goalie Ramage saves a header

Nelson, was brought in. At Swansea they played some really great stuff, winning 5-2 Phillips getting that record. A great career —most of his goals were scored for Ipswich. Only 9000 came along for the next home match against Rotherham, and the many who stayed away missed one of the most powerful shots ever seen at Brisbane Road. Ted Phillips picked up a ball on the halfway line and hammered it home past United goalie Morritt. Phillips added another later to make it 2-1. He had now scored ten goals in the eleven matches and looked well on the way to Johnston's record of 36. Rotherham at this time were top with eleven points and this win gave Orient ten points. But the form didn't last. They had a break for the third round Cup-tie in which they beat Barnsley through Phillips and Gregory. In the League they were beaten by Palace (with their star studded team) and by Newcastle and drew with Coventry.

FENTON GOES

After a couple more bad performances the team at a low ebb, were beaten hollow at home by Swindon on 19th December 3-0. A few days later Benny Fenton was dismissed and Les Gore became caretaker-manager. His first job was to sign Dave Metchick for £10,000 from Fulham. Metchick made his debut on Brisbane Road's snow covered pitch against Charlton, and hammered home a 25 yarder. Orient never looked back, winning 4-2 with goals from Phillips 2, and Dave Dunmore, but they suffered four more defeats soon after. The board of directors were getting worried and on the 14th January 65 Dave Sexton was appointed manager. The son of well known boxer Archie Sexton, Dave came to Orient via Chelsea, where he was coach for three years. Dave played for the Orient in 56/7 and scored the club's first goal in the second division. He moved on to Brighton, then to Crystal Palace. He started his playing career with Luton Town and later moved to West Ham. For the trip to Crystal Palace Sexton brought in goalkeeper George Ramage and Jeff Harris, but still the team were beaten 1-0. They were now at the bottom of the division on 22 points. On 13th March, playing for the O's reserves, was Peter Allen, in his very first game for an Orient team (against Southend Reserves). Peter, only 17 years of age, played very well and the match ended 2-2.

Just before the transfer deadline Sexton tried to sign Norwich forward Jim Oliver. He raised the money by selling Ted Phillips to Luton—Phillips had lost all his goalscoring flair—but at the last minute Oliver decided to join Brighton. (He did manage to sign another Norwich forward, Colin Shaw). The relegation battle was still on; as April approached Orient were right in the thick of it. Their performances at the end were not good, though they made sure of staying in the division with a goalless draw at Bolton. The club had an interesting idea about summer football, and they issued 6000 fans with forms for their views. The results were as follows:

Forms issued   6000
In favour   4026
Against   526

Dave Sexton jarred faithful fans when he told them the list of players who weren't to be retained for the new season. They were: Sid Bishop, Stan Charlton, Terry McDonald, Mike Pinner, George Ramage, Dave Dunmore, Gerry Ward and Mike Hollow—quite a lot of experience and skill to be cast off in one lump. During the summer some veteran players were signed, and young Peter Allen moved up after playing quite a few games last season in the reserves. Sexton was very impressed with him. Young Paul Went signed apprentice forms.

THE BIG DROP

For the 65/6 season Orient came out on to the turf against Huddersfield wearing a selection from the new range designed by David Sexton: white shorts and blue shirts with a matching white sash over the chest. Three more defeats followed and Sexton, getting a bit worried, brought in goalkeeper Vic Rouse and young defender Paul Went (for his League debut), only 15 years and 10 months, Orient's youngest ever League player. The visitors were Preston North End. Colin Flatt scored twice, but it wasn't enough, the match ended 2-2. In the 53rd minute the very first Orient substitute was called upon; Joe Elwood came on for the injured Jimmy McGeorge. This was the season when the substitute rule was introduced, (a substitute could only come on for an injured player, approved by the referee). Young Went had a great game and came very close to scoring with a fine shot which was just over the bar.

Jimmy Scott the skipper, at 20 years old, was the youngest captain out of the 92 clubs, and the side he now led, away at Birmingham was also one of the youngest in the League. He scored both the goals in that match to make a 2-2 draw. When Birmingham came to Leyton, the team did very well to beat them 2-1. However, two defeats came very swiftly afterwards, and Sexton went out to sign John Smith from Coventry. In his very first game, against

Open day at Orient, 5.8.65. First team squad bombard manager Dave Sexton

Bolton, Smith hit a terrific goal late on to give us two priceless points. Sexton made some more changes, dropping Smith back and putting centre half Gordon Ferry in the forward line. Even then the team didn't look very sharp, losing 3-0 against Wolves. The team went six matches without a win. They picked up a point at Jimmy Hill's top of the table Coventry, Harry Gregory scoring a late equaliser in front of 20,110.

TRUSTY GORE

The team lost very heavily home and away. They were on the bottom of the division and looked set for relegation even by January. Andy Nelson had left the club to join Plymouth Argyle, and following defeats by Bristol City and at Manchester City, Dave Sexton decided to quit the club. It was left yet again to Les Gore to take the helm and he tried a more attacking plan. Under Sexton, including last season, the forwards did not score more than two goals in a first team game, and quite a few of the players he decided to let go, would have seen us in a more respectable position. Colin Flatt had lost touch and seemed too slow for League football after his bright

CRISIS, 20.11.66. Defeats and declining receipts cause the meeting to be called ▲
O's v Manchester City, 7.5.66. City's Bell (no 8) scores their 2nd goal ▼

spell. By March the team looked doomed. Gore sold David Webb to Southampton for about £23,000, and bought George O'Brien, 29 year old forward from Southampton, Dick Le Flem from Middlesborough, and young Mike Jones from Chelsea. The renewed team made a last ditch effort to save themselves and had a fine 3-1 victory at Derby County, with goals from Metchick 2, and Le Flem. But Orient's fate was sealed on 18th April, a Monday evening.

One of the lowest home gates ever, 2286, were huddled around the rain swamped pitch. It looked like a pond, yet the referee blew his whistle and Orient waded through the storm to take a 2-0 lead, goals Terry Price scuttled into the net. Amazingly, the referee decided to continue and awarded Middlesborough a penalty, which was converted. In the second half O's were attacking the deep end. By this time it had become impossible to move there and it would have been a miracle if they had scored. At the other end, Middlesborough were pre-occupied putting in two more of their own, to win 3-2 and plunge us into the third division. Orient won five games during the whole season, notching 23 points, 10 behind Middlesborough, who were also relegated. A number of players deserve special praise for fine efforts during this unlucky campaign. Gordon Ferry for his calm and clever defensive work. David Webb was excellent as a tough tackling defender which led to his transfer to Southampton. Peter Allen also showed star quality. O's had completed a full circle back to division three. What was the main factor in the poor showing of the team? A lack of zip up front and the fact that too many experienced players were unloaded by Dave Sexton at the start. Les Gore, for the sixth time, had taken over the managerial spot, but it was just a bit too late for him to save the day.

EXTINCTION?

1966/7 was Orient's season for lime-light and headlines, for their ill fortune mostly. In June Dick Graham was appointed as manager. Graham was something of a sergeant-major figure. He had been goalkeeper for Crystal Palace and later manager, and it was the belief at Orient that a tough no-nonsense type was needed to get to grips with the chronic situation.

Calamity struck before the season started. Graham's old back complaint was giving him trouble and he was in hospital when things got underway. He put Cliff Holton and Brian Whitehouse, two of his first signings (from Charlton in exchange for Gregory) that he knew from his Palace and Charlton days, in charge of team matters. This put Les Gore in an odd position, as he appeared to be the only one who could properly take charge in such circumstances. The team for the opening match at Oldham was chosen after consultations at the hospital between Graham, Holton and Whitehouse. Although Metchick scored a good goal, they lost 3-1. There was more enthusiasm in their performance against Scunthorpe in the first home tie, and tricky Terry Price, coming in for injured O'Brien scored in the 3-1 victory (Metchick and Whitehouse). But alas, the squad, who ought to have been good enough for the third division, didn't show this spirit often, and a list of injuries was not helping matters. They went the next six games without a win, and an unlucky League Cup exit, 1-0 at Brighton, added to the barren patch.

A splendid overhead-kick goal by Cliff Holton against Swansea put that right, but the crowds had now dwindled. Young Ron Willis had settled down quite well in goal, and he was normally chosen in spite of Vic Rouse returning to fitness. The decline resumed and before the next match at Colchester, it was becoming too obvious that the club was entering another financial crisis. When they dismissed Les Gore, Dick Graham was quoted in one newspaper as saying: 'Put it down to a difference in policy if you like.' But a few days earlier trainer Dave Clarke and Jack Tonner the groundsman had been fired, and six players put on the transfer list: John Smith, Dave Metchick, Dennis Sorrell, Dick Le Flem, Gordon Ferry and Eddie Farmer. (There was one significant signing: Paul Went moved up from apprentice to full-time professional). At the time it was emphasised that the trainer and groundsman had left for other than financial reasons. Clark, a former Orient centre-half and only taken on as trainer for this season, was quoted in the *Daily Mirror*: 'You could say I had a personal disagreement with the manager. I am very disappointed.'

Some of these measures were imperative; the club was losing money at a rate that couldn't continue—Dick Graham: 'This is an economic necessity, the slide won't be stopped by getting further and further into debt. The club have got to adjust themselves to the fact that they are no longer in the first division.'

On the 29th October this notice appeared in the programme for the match at home against Watford:

It became a sort of soccer Peyton Place... a continuing story that must have left every Orient supporter wondering what the next instalment would bring. The headlines about recent events inside the club screamed from the national newspapers. You felt almost cheated if you picked up your paper in the morning and found nothing new had happened at Leyton's stadium the previous day...The news has been accurate. Some of the interpretation has been wide of the mark. We feel loyal Orient fans should know our position and, equally important, our policy. Above all, we want to emphasise, THERE IS NO CRISIS...

We need £1500 a week to pay our way. That means an average gate of 10,000 for each home match. At the moment, attendances at Leyton Stadium are down to the 5000 mark. It means that the cash coming through the turnstiles has fallen to around £1300 every two weeks. Reports that the club is around £100,000 in the red, and that we are losing up to £500 a week are substantially correct.

That is why we are now making moves to put the house in order...New faces, new ideas and a strengthened team is our policy for the future. A policy that will mean a bigger part than ever before in Orient's history for young players. Players like Ron Willis and Paul Went are already proving that youngsters have a better chance of coming through quickly with Orient than they would have with some of the bigger clubs.

We intend to give absolute priority to helping schoolboy and youth players. Schools and youth organisations who would like to use Orient's ground facilities will be given a warm welcome. Come along and meet manager Dick Graham and the players. We can help each other. That is our position—and our policy. We feel Orient is a club with a successful future. We hope you feel that way too.

The team's play reflected the strife and the problems, and the following defeats at QPR and Swindon they were second from bottom. Some relief came in an entertaining Cup-tie against Lowestoft Town, Orient winning 2-1.

On the previous Sunday the Club held what is now known as their famous 'Pass the Bucket' meeting.

This was a heart-rending experience for all who held the O's dear. There had been crises before, as in 1906, 30, 32 and in the Second World War, and now their very existence was again in the balance. There to lead the fight was director Arthur Page, who put in plain terms what we were up against. Page was the man who had written to all the directors a few months earlier suggesting that the club was insolvent. The response was so disappointing that he took matters into his own hands.

After the speeches, things began gloom-

Despite a gloomy start offers and donations soon start pouring in

ily. Several criticisms came from the audience, some sensible, some not so sensible, and one felt that if things went on like this the outlook would be bleak. But suddenly the mood seemed to change and genuine offers of help came from people. A bucket was passed round and sixpences, pennies, halfcrowns and notes were tossed into it. The total amount may have been minimal in relation to the club's needs, but there were offers of a more lasting kind. Arthur Page was moved by this—if the grandads could spare some of their pensions and the schoolboys some of their pocket money, there was obviously a general feeling of

concern for the club, and the effort to save the Orient was worth making. They decided to set up several small money-making schemes; it really seemed that if they all willed hard enough the tide could be made to turn yet. Back on the pitch the lads went 5 matches without defeat, bringing 7 points out of 10. Brentwood put us out of the Cup in a replay. After Christmas there was a revival and 4 matches, 3 away, were won—and they did particularly well from now on, though results fell back later. Graham made more signings and there was now enough experience in the side to pull them out of trouble. Over

Easter they soared away from danger with 5 points out of six. They had a far more confident look now and the final weeks of the season were quite a contrast. Graham made a significant change by pulling Mick Jones out of the defence; he went forward and captain Whitehouse moved into the right-back berth. They were still not completely safe, and had a tricky game at Mansfield on 22nd April. The point that put away the fears was earned by Mick Jones with a late, lone goal at Walsall on the 6th May.

It had been an eventful term. The supporters and fans held a second meeting on 26th February and Arthur Page, now chairman of the club (Harry Zussman stayed on the board), revealed that one of the Orient's more affluent supporters had given £5000 with no strings attached. Although the general situation had improved slightly there was still an uphill struggle ahead. A larger than usual Derby draw was organised that proved in the event, not as successful as had been hoped. In June Paul Went was sold to Charlton for £26,000. People helped in ways both big and small, and one in particular deserves a mention. We still owed £4000 of Metchick's transfer fee to Fulham, and their Chairman Tommy Trinder told Arthur Page not to worry about it. Page's reply was quoted in the papers: 'He shall be the first one settled when we get some money.' A millionaire, Ron Blundell, offered to pay off all debts on condition that he was given complete control of the club. Page replied that: 'As we are a happy club with loyal supporters my board and I decided we didn't want someone from outside to take over.'

As we have seen, many young players had been given a chance in the first team. Some were pushed in prematurely perhaps, like Tony Ackerman and Terry Street, but others, like Barry Fry, Tommy Goodgame and Ken Woodward, were good honest triers, if a trifle short on class. Three trainers had left, and Barry Fry was made trainer towards the end. The team finished fourteenth, Cliff Holton topping the scorers list on 17. The reserves, who had withdrawn from the Combination last year, were now scrapped altogether (they played in the Midweek League this season). Fifteen full-timers only started the 67/8 season, plus a squad of apprentices, and there was only one newcomer, Tom Anderson the forward, formerly of Watford. And from here on the club was Orient, not Leyton Orient.

Of course, it was hoped that with such a small professional staff the players would escape injury, and it was typical of the club's luck that Jones was ruled out with an eye injury he received in the very first match. Anderson had also taken a minor knock and for the fixture at Torquay two Colts players, John Still and Tommy Taylor, 17 and 15 respectively, were drafted into the first team. Torquay proved to be too experienced for them and won 2-0. Cliff Holton was injured in the League Cup-tie versus Gillingham, who won 3-1 at Leyton Stadium. The problems had hit us much sooner than expected and Dick Graham had to act quickly. Between 29th August and 1st September he added five players to the staff, all of them included in the third match at Reading, the new look side going down by 4-2, of the new men Massey and Halom looked the best. A midweek thrashing by five goals at Walsall with Willis back in goal put them near the bottom of the table. In the first week of October, there were two major signings: Dave Harper, a player Graham had long admired, from Swindon, and Vic Halom, who had been back at Charlton only five days after his loan period. Rumours were still going round that Orient were near to going under, but it was surely a significant factor that the club were spending some money on players; the situation had, if only slightly, eased. The League position and several newspaper reports forecasting the fold-up made O's supporters think otherwise, however. A

Football 'money-boxes' help the "Save the Orient Fund"

particularly worrying aspect were the attendances, reaching a new low of 3,000 to 4,000. Following a defeat at the stadium by Northampton, the game for the home match versus Oldham Athletic was the lowest of the season, with huge gaps on the terraces. Amid all this there was one ray of light. A set of very talented youngsters were playing for the Orient Colts and some of these were obvious players of the future. If Orient could keep going, then there was certainly a future to look forward to. Another bright spot was when Terry Mancini walked into the club's offices and asked for a trial at the end of October. He had just returned from South Africa where he played for the Port Elizabeth club. Before that he had played for Watford. It wasn't long before everyone at Brisbane Road realised he had done us a

favour by coming that day.

The lowest ebb had been reached in every way against Oldham, but the following match at home to Barrow was the first sign that the pendulum was starting to swing back our way. Many fans will look back at this fixture of the 11th November as the first step up from the depths. Mancini at centre half crowned his debut with a driving header, and how those injury depleted O's fought, to win 4-2. The fighting spirit still burned in the next match at home to Reading which was won 1-0. Mancini, who had an outstanding match was rewarded when he trudged off at the end, for Graham was waiting with the forms for him to sign. He had seen enough in just two games to know that there was no need to keep him on trial. But the team were still only three from the bottom. (It was good to hear at this time that the idea of moving from Leyton stadium to Basildon was now definitely off, like the suggestions of a Romford and Orient merger earlier. Not so good was the news that Waltham Forest council had turned down requests for a £50,000 loan—though the council did say it was not in their legal power to grant such a loan).

The biggest blow came when Cliff Holton was forced to retire because of leg and vein trouble. 'Bigg Cliff' will always be remembered for the great life-saving act he performed for the club in 66/7. Another meeting was held at the ground on Sunday 21st January and the signs that financial matters were improving were obvious, but on the field results continued to be unpredictable.

BLOOMFIELD REPLACES GRAHAM

Dick Graham dropped a bombshell by resigning during the last week in February. He had been upset by the directors' decision not to give him sufficient cash to buy a new player or two. Before the next game the directors had appointed Jimmy Bloomfield as player-manager. Bloomfield, 34, was best known for his long association with Arsenal, and this was to be his first shot at a managerial job. The placings at the foot of division three before this match were:

	Played	Points
Mansfield Town	31	26
ORIENT	28	24
Scunthorpe	33	24
Grimsby	31	20

The matches in hand were obviously in our favour, they had only to be clear of the bottom three, and not four as usual, because Peterborough were automatically relegated owing to certain irregularities. Strikers Vic Halom and Roy Massey were hitting some reasonable form and new man John Key looked useful. They did not concede a goal in the three Easter games against Mansfield, plus a 1-0 victory over high riding Oxford United and had practic-

ally made matters safe with six games still to go, and these final six yielded six points. Two more youngsters were blooded in this spell: Dennis Rofe, a sprightly defender and Steve Bowtell, the tall, slim goalkeeper. The final position in the League was nineteenth. Before leaving 67/8 we should recall two other things. At Christmas, with the financial troubles at their height, the players, led by skipper Brian Wood, declined the offer of a Christmas bonus, to keep the club's expenses as low as possible—a commendable action. Around this time the club was prepared to listen to offers for any of their playing staff, bar Goddard. This was because of an outstanding debt. And so the term closed, a season which, by the way, saw the O's in the new colours: red shirts and red shorts.

FAIR HOPE, BUT LING'RING FOOT

There was considerable reason to be optimistic at the opening of the 68/9 campaign: a fresh, go-ahead young manager to guide the team, and ex-England international signed, Peter Brabrook, a fighting squad that had pulled them through a worrying season, and a bunch of Colts maturing all the time. The club was also recruiting a reserve side for the Midweek League. The team looked good in pre-season friendlies, so now for the real thing. The first test was at home to Tommy Docherty's newly relegated Rotherham. The crowd certainly enjoyed Orient's skilful attacking, Peter Brabrook making electrifying runs on the left wing, and Malcolm Slater doing likewise down the right. They drew 3-3, and Tommy Docherty paid this compliment: 'They were as good as most teams we met in division two last season.' The next match was a League Cup-tie at Gillingham and they played so cleverly that Bloomfield wrote in the next programme, 'We looked in a different class from Rotherham and Gillingham.' Both games were drawn but the promise was there, and the problems of the previous season seemed 100 years ago. Orient were the last third division team to lose, going eleven games before tasting defeat, setting up an Orient post-war record. Then the club suffered what was almost certainly their biggest setback of the campaign. Against Oldham at Leyton in September Peter Brabrook had to leave the pitch with a tendon injury and did not play any more first team soccer all season.

Results and performances took a turn for the worse from here onwards. To add to the troubles John Key, the experienced winger who might have been expected to take Braybrook's place, suffered a similar injury and he too did not play again all season. The team slid from near the top to three quarters down the table, though things seemed to improve around Christmas. A new striker was signed during the holiday, Barry Dyson from Watford. At the start of the Easter session they were one place below halfway, but they failed to gain a single point over the holiday. Where was the style of football that Jimmy Bloomfield had instilled in them at the start? A fifth defeat on the trot, at Oldham, fellow strugglers, plunged O's deep into trouble. The early promotion hopefuls were now looking like relegation probables. With two matches remaining these were the facts:

	Played	Points
19th ORIENT	44	38
Shrewsbury	42	38
Hartlepool	44	38
Mansfield	41	35
Oldham	45	34
Crewe	43	32

In the final match, at home to Shrewsbury, they still needed to win to make quite certain. Shrewsbury needed the points too, but had games in hand. There was quite an atmosphere in the stadium on the night, a week before all had seemed lost. There were some fans who were confident they could do it, but few would have forecast they would do it by four clear goals. They were safe and about 100 supporters did a knees-up round the centre circle and in the

Orient v Roma (friendly) 4.5.70.
Terry Mancini (left) exchanges pennants

street after the match. The joy was such you might have thought they had won the Cup. How a side as talented as this got itself into such a mess, heaven knows. Surely now the club could look forward to better times. Both chairman Arthur Page and manager Jimmy Bloomfield thought so. Barry Dyson topped the scorers list with 10, and Terry Mancini, the captain in succession to Whitehouse and Wood, was the only player to appear in all League, FA Cup and League Cup games. During the 68/9 campaign Waltham Forest council turned down Orient's plea for a reduced rent.

Jimmy Bloomfield decided to concentrate solely on his managerial duties for the 69/70 season—he certainly ended his playing career on a high note. His display in that final match was undoubtedly one of his best for Orient, but he was in his mid thirties now. He made two major signings, and there was good news concerning Peter Brabrook. At last his injury had cleared up and he was to be included in the team to visit Rochdale for the opening.

THEY GLORY IN ORIENT

It was better than could have been wished, a 3-0 victory with Orient too good in all departments, and on 30th August a significant change was made in the line-up. 18 year old youth and reserve goalpoacher, Barrie Fairbrother was included in the attack against Mansfield. Barrie, who had scored more goals for the youth sides than any other player ever before, made a great debut and scored the only goal of the game to put Orient in fifth position. The lads continued to play well and the notable factor about the first quarter of the season was that Orient kept meeting clubs who were highly placed in the League. That they won most of these matches was proof of their right to be promotion candidates.

Before the next match Jimmy Bloomfield went to Crystal Palace to buy back Mark Lazarus for a fee of about £7,000. Lazarus plus his strength and power would undoubtedly add to the team's chances of promotion. After three victories they were challenging strongly in fourth position. Dismissal from the Cup did not unduly worry the team and they plodded on efficiently and constantly. By the New Year they were top of the division. Luton were faltering at this time and the top four were Orient, Luton, Barnsley, Reading. Bury and Tranmere were the next clubs to be outplayed. Tranmere were particularly fortunate to lose by only two goals. This was an unlucky day for skipper Terry Mancini who broke a bone in his leg, and for the away trip to Reading Orient had to do without him. Mancini had now played in 120 consecutive first team games, 105 League, 9 FA Cup and 6 League Cup. Bloomfield moved young Tommy Taylor into the centre-half spot and brought Dickie Plume in, as Dave Harper was still unfit. The side were hitting some fine form now despite Mancini's absence, and the division table looked like this on the 14th March:

	P	W	D	L	F	A	P
1st ORIENT	34	18	11	5	49	25	47
Bristol Rovers	37	17	13	7	69	46	47
Brighton	38	19	9	10	48	32	47
Luton	35	17	11	7	60	36	45
Reading	36	17	10	9	62	54	44

But the battle was far from over. For once transfer deadline came round without the club having to make any desperate last minute signings. They entered the tough Easter programme and took four points from a possible six. This kept them on top of goal average, though joint top Rovers and Brighton had played more games. On the evening of the FA Cup final they met Rochdale and the Lancashire club led 2-0 with just 12 minutes to go—were they faltering at this late stage? It seemed so, but they managed to escape an equaliser with only three minutes to go.

Promotion was guaranteed on the Wednesday with a 1-0 win at Bradford City. The goal was headed home by Bullock after a fine run and centre by Lazarus. It was a happy journey back to London for players and supporters alike. They clinched the championship on Saturday 25th April, beating Shrewsbury Town 1-0, Lazarus heading the goal. In the final League game, at home to Gillingham. O's were applauded on to the pitch by Gillingham and then did a lap of honour. After the match the team were presented with the division three trophy by Charlton Athletic's chairman Mr. Glikstein. Thousands of fans on the pitch, terracing and in the grandstand joined in singing 'You'll never walk alone'.

It is difficult to know where to begin when handing out the accolades. Arthur Page must take much of the credit for leading the fight back. He was helped by his fellow directors and loyal supporters and

Ray Goddard, Stephen Bowtell and Tom Walley in training

followers. The financial improvement had been partly due to the young go-ahead pools scheme organiser Brian Blower, who succeeded former player Johnny Hartburn in 67 after being his assistant. Jimmy Bloomfield did a marvellous job, his efforts and sensible management of the team earned him the honour of being elected third division manager of the season. That loyal servant Peter Angell, the club trainer, worked hard and was a good man in handling players. Physiotherapist Charlie Simpson was invaluable to the team. And there is one man we must not forget, ex-manager Dick Graham, for it was he who had the manager's seat in the dark days of 66/7. Arthur Page called a celebration meeting on Sunday 26th April. It was well attended and in complete contrast to those desperate Sunday gatherings we have recalled; it was optimism all the way. Page and Bloomfield thanked everyone concerned in the revival and Bloomfield stated his aim—division one. An important appointment during the season was Mr. Len Cheesewright, made full-time youth manager after 12 years with the club part-time. Mickey Bullock was the top scorer on 19, followed by Fairbrother on 13, then Lazarus 7. It is interesting that they used less players in this season, only sixteen, than in any other before.

Jimmy Bloomfield gave a vote of confidence to the lads by not making a single change during the summer. Sheffield United were first customers at Leyton and Lazarus put in two to make a 3-1 victory. The team continued to play fairly well, gaining five

Trainer Peter Angell

points from the first four games (1 win, 3 draws). It wasn't until October that the real slump began. From third they slipped to below halfway, and the first venture into the transfer market came on 14th October. Tommy Taylor, the highly promising starlet, moved to West Ham for £78,000, some of this being eaten up buying Peter Bennett as part of the deal (about £15,000). On the same day, Gordon Riddick was bought from Charlton for £10,000. It was about this time that Dave Harper learned that his knee injury would not allow him to play any more League soccer. Few fans will forget his spirit, especially during the releg-

ation struggles of 68/9. The team got into a rut after November, going 13 games without a win. The main problem was obvious. In defence they were reasonably sound but the forwards had failed to score in ten of their first 23 games.

However, they made a new effort and out of the next six matches they won four and drew two scoring four goals and conceding none. A 1-0 victory at Middlesborough put them up to just under halfway. There were ten matches remaining and only an average amount of success would have seen the club finish in a respectable position. Alas, it was not to be for, in a very dismal spell, they did not win a single game, drew only three and lost seven. They finished seventeenth place, scoring in all a paltry 29, the lowest in their entire history. Lazarus was the top scorer with 6 (another all time low).

Nevertheless, the club had seen out their first term back in the second division without many relegation worries, and perhaps the most pleasing aspect of 70/1 was the healthy state of the finances. Incoming transfer fees outweighed the outgoing fees and gates weren't too bad considering the lack of goals. They had come a long way from the shipwreck days of 66. Arthur Page had matters under control at boardroom level, and Jimmy Bloomfield was sowing the seeds of a prosperous playing future. Jimmy Bloomfield had made a notable signing in June, 19 year old striker Ian Bowyer from Manchester City for a fee of £25,000.

PETCHEY REPLACES BLOOMFIELD

At the end of June the club lost another manager. Leicester City had shown interest in Bloomfield, and eventually got their man. His departure took place while Arthur Page was abroad on holiday, and on hearing of it, he was, understandably, not pleased. Bloomfield was under contract and this had not run out. Page wanted more discussions on some form of compensation from Leic-

At the Races, Phil Hoadley borrows Paul Harris's binoculars. The day before their
FA Cup match with Arsenal

ester but, apparently, vice-chairman Neville Ovenden had passed the move. There was a fairly amicable settlement though Ovenden resigned from the board. There had to be a search and time was short. There were many names linked with the vacant post, and just before the final announcement the number had been whittled down to two by the general Press. They were Palace coach George Petchey (a former West Ham, Palace and QPR player), who had coached Palace through some of their most successful seasons, and ex-Orient player Cyril Lea, who had proved his worth as Ipswich Town's coach. On the 12th July they appointed George Petchey. Arthur Page was quoted as saying at the time: 'I am sure we have picked the right man. Petchey was chosen bec-

ause of his fine record for Palace and we feel sure he will do well at Orient.'

Petchey's first buy was a very modest one. He snapped up Palace's Len Tomkins on a trial basis. Then he signed 25 year old John Sewell on a free transfer from Palace on 5th August. Sewell had captained Palace in the recent successful seasons. A young winger Peter Johnson also joined early in the summer. The early results of 71/2 were rather similar to those of the previous term and the side failed to score in three matches, and after six games only one had been won. Petchey decided it was time to add to his playing staff and on 3rd October he signed Phil Hoadley from his former club, Palace (£30,000). Nobody during the crisis would have dreamed such fees would

Despite winning at the races, Orient lose to Arsenal (19.3.72)

soon be in order as those for Bowyer and Hoadley. Hoadley, a sturdy 19 year old defender, was highly regarded by Petchey, and he was versatile, doing a good job at full back, centre-forward and midfield, and filling in as a striker if required. On 10th October an old favourite left the club, Terry 'Henry' Mancini. The 'Skipper' was transferred to QPR for an approximate fee of £25,000. He never quite seemed to regain his best form since his injury against Tranmere in 70, but he certainly did for QPR in later seasons—holding his own in their first division side. Peter Bennett, who had be-

come a firm favourite with the Brisbane Road crowd for his quiet efficient play, was appointed team captain.

One victory from the next four matches shows the general trend of the results, a just below average of points for games. Petchey made another shrewd move on 6th December, signing Tom Walley, a Welsh international midfield player from Watford. On 28th December Mick Jones moved to Charlton for £10,000. Jones came to Orient in the latter part of the 65/6 term and performed consistently, giving always of his best. He was well liked by the fans, turning

Gerry Queen, Derrick Downing, Terry Brisly, Mickey Bullock and Bobby Arber in training

out 223 times in the League, 15 times in the FA Cup and 10 times in the League Cup, and was a regular member of the 69/70 promotion side.

There was a nice blend in the team now and the side that lined up against Wrexham in the third round had a look of class about it. Petchey was carefully improving things, not rushing into any signings but coolly waiting for the right man at the right price. Wrexham posed problems, and the tie was well into the second half and still not a goal in sight despite heavy Orient pressure. Orient eventually broke the ice, though it took a twice taken penalty kick by Dyson to do it. Fairbrother and Bowyer added further goals in the final flourish. The FA fourth round tie with Leicester created great interest. Bloomfield being with Orient such a short time back was one reason, another was Ian Bowyer, Bloomfield's last signing for us, who would be eager to do well. Also trainer Peter Angell had turned

down an offer from Bloomfield to team up with him at Leicester and must have had feelings as he travelled down with the team. Urged on by a continuous 'Orient, Orient' chant they played magnificently, and the 2-0 defeat made Jimmy Bloomfield's pre-match quote, 'Sorry Orient, you'll have to go', look a bit sick. Afterwards he sportingly acknowledged, 'They deserved to win'.

In the fifth round came Dave Sexton's Chelsea stars to do battle. Both Sexton and Petchey were living in Brighton then and often used to travel to London together, discussing each others' teams' problems, but not for this match. Chelsea dominated the early period and took the lead with a smart goal by David Webb. In the 36th minute Peter Osgood notched a second from Cooke's corner. The turning point came just before half-time when Phil Hoadley rocketed one past Bonetti. Orient were level just four minutes after returning. Chelsea seemed ruffled. The eager O's chased every ball but it was not just enthusiasm. Hoadley, Walley, Rofe and Bullock all showed skilful touches. As time was running out it looked like a replay at Stamford Bridge, but then Bullock controlled a high ball and turned it sideways to Tom Walley. The shrewd Welshman sent a superb ball through the middle for Bowyer and Fairbrother clipped it into the net. The stadium exploded and Fairbrother (Barrie the beard) was mobbed. Since then people wanting to draw attention to the unmarked Fairbrother shout 'Give it to Flash'. Unfortunately in the sixth round Arsenal held out to win by one disputed goal.

Back to the more mundane fare after the glamour of the Cup. Points were again needed and the Easter Fixtures gave them four points out of a possible six. Any fears of relegation vanished with a 1-0 win over Watford on 22nd April. The final League placing of seventeenth was not good enough though the FA Cup made up for it. George Petchey could look back on his first season with satisfaction. A strong addition to the club was Mr. Arthur Rowe as general adviser, on 24th January. Rowe, an ex-Tottenham player, became famous as the Spurs manager in the early 50s. He was the brain behind their push and run side which was so successful. Later he managed Palace and Petchey was a colleague of Rowe's there. Ian Bowyer was the highest scorer with 15 League and 2 FA goals.

Orient could not break out of the mould that had held them for the past two seasons. There followed defeats at Hull and at home to Bristol City. The second round of the League Cup at first division Wolves was a stiff task indeed. They didn't manage to win, but they certainly gave Wolves a scare. Petchey signed Gerry Queen from Palace for £50,000, and he had a very quiet debut against QPR though the game was splendid entertainment and 2-2 result was just about right. Fairbrother and Downing scored cracking goals—all under the watchful eye of England team manager Sir Alf Ramsey. More performances like this would surely see a swift rise up the table. It did not materialise. They drew six consecutive matches. Injury problems made things worse, and the run extended to nine games without a win. The League placings was all too familiar, just above the danger zone. Talent there was, and if an injection of confidence was what the team required then the events of Saturday 11th November should have provided it. That day, Orient visited leaders Burnley, the last unbeaten team in the divisions, and beat them 2-1. If that kind of showing against the top side was typical of Orient, then so was the result the following week. They travelled to lowly Swindon, with a depleted team through injuries, and lost 3-1. This was how results continued into the new year. Ricky Heppolette was signed from Preston two days before Christmas for a sizeable fee, and there was a need for defensive reinforcements. The sole priority now had once more to be League points. It was the game at home to Blackpool that was the beginning of better things, a 2-0 success, and this sparked off an excellent run of home wins, seven in succession. Fairbrother notched five goals and was showing some of his best form for the club. This home run was not sustained and during the same period they lost seven consecutive away games.

A Sunday meeting was once again held in the grandstand, on 25th February, the day after the four goal victory over Villa, and revealed plenty of optimism. The final game was drawn at home to Sunderland, who won the Cup five days later. The final League position of fifteenth was respectable enough after the earlier worries and the alarming number of injuries. Tom Walley appeared in only eight full League matches and only twice as substitute (one of these against Sunderland). Team captain Peter Bennett had two lengthy spells out and Fairbrother, Heppolette, Arber and Harris were among others with periods off through injury. But it was also a season of promise.

Young Malcolm Linton came out of his first season well, showing himself to be a no nonsense defender. Teenager John Lewis came on twice as substitute and more established men like Queen, Heppolette and Downing had proved good boys. Barrie Fairbrother's form in the later stages of the season was a revelation. He was sharp, alert, and quick to seize his chances. He finished as the club's top scorer with 11.

For three seasons now, Orient had finished in almost identical position in the table. There was considerable speculation about the coming 73/4 term. It was generally reckoned that it was going to be something of a dog fight in division three. The famous Charlton brothers were setting off on their managerial careers: Jackie at Middlesborough, Bobby at Preston North End. Big spending Crystal Palace relegated from division one with Malcolm Allison in charge, were fancied for a quick return, as were Don Howe's West Brom, and others in the betting were FA Cup winners Sunderland, Aston Villa, Nott'm Forest and Fulham. According to many of the so-called experts, hot favourites for relegation were Orient and Swindon Town, with Cardiff and Carlisle close behind. Football's powers-that-be brought a new ruling into operation. Instead of two up and two down between first, second and third divisions it would now be three up and three down. This would be too much for Orient, so many dismal Jimmies thought.

Paul Harris

So Near: Their Story

There was a fluency about Orient's play at the start of 73/4 that was exciting; it was in the 'push and run' style that Arthur Rowe made famous at Tottenham. The visiting Blackpool side were shaken by their class. (The seasiders lost 3-2). The following match at home to Middlesborough finished goalless but was a highly entertaining affair. 'Boro were sixth in the table after a 2-2 draw at Aston Villa. Bristol City led the division at this stage, 3 points ahead of Orient, and high praise was showering in from every manager in opposition to us.

During these early games a new name emerged on the first team scene, teenager Bobby Fisher. His first full League appearance was at Bolton (having twice been substitute) and he demonstrated remarkable coolness and skill for such a tender age. Another experiment was the move of Phil Hoadley to centre-half to the exclusion of Malcolm Linton. Mike O'Shaughnessy, an 18 year old, made his debut in place of injured Ray Goddard at Hull City and did quite well. Cup progress was made with a very comfortable 2-0 home victory over third division Blackburn Rovers. The next few League games showed Orient at their most brilliant. But George Petchey sprung a surprise the week before when, on Wednesday 17th October he once again went to his former club Palace to sign the experienced keeper John Jackson for £25,000, and the defender Bill Roffey for a bargain £5,000. Earlier the same day Orient's Ian Bowyer, who had been in dispute with the club over wages, was sold to Nottingham for a reported £40,000.

And then the team were held 1-1 in the

O's v Sunderland, Barrie Fairbrother scores O's 2nd goal

◀ O's v Bournemouth

Bullock scores O's first goal against Cardiff City

third round of the League Cup by York City, who were going great guns in the third division, and Preston North End took a point at Brisbane Road in a 2-2 draw. It was suddenly noticable that Orient, though still playing attractive stuff, were allowing inferior sides to steal points. York knocked Orient out of the League Cup in the replay scoring the winner in the dying seconds of extra time. The team held second or third position for several weeks, but after a one goal success at Millwall there were two rude shocks in store. Both Cardiff and Carlisle came to Brisbane Road and left with two points. By the New Year, injuries were mounting up, and Jackson, Allen and Queen were kept out. It was a depleted side that beat Bournemouth in the third round of the FA Cup 2-1 (Barrie Fairbroth-

er). An important point was gained at Blackpool through a Bullock penalty and two points were scraped from Sunderland at home when Gerry Queen returned after six matches, netted the first, and Fairbrother the second. In the fourth round of the FA Cup they played at Portsmouth. Almost fifty coachloads of supporters left Brisbane Road, in an exodus to Pompey, but the match was not up to normal Cup-tie standards and no goals were scored. Portsmouth dumped us out of the FA Cup in the second replay at Selmhurst Park, 2-0.

At Palace they managed a draw despite Ricky Heppolette going off with a bad shoulder injury, and 10,365 saw a below par Orient against Oxford. It took a great diving header from Derrick Downing in injury time to salvage a point. Just as the

    O's v Aston Villa. O's bring on flowers for the ladies in this last vital match ▶

ORIENT

John Jackson, Malcolm Linton, John Boyle and Paul Harris watch while their team-mates battle Villa

crunch was coming, Orient seemed to be faltering. Fellow promotion candidates Luton Town beat them 3-1. Luton were holding on to the second place but Nott'm Forest, Carlisle, West Brom, Blackpool and even fast finishers Sunderland were converging on Orient. The Easter period yielded three points from three matches. The top positions at this crucial stage were:

	Pl.	P.
Middlesborough	40	61
Luton	39	47
Blackpool	40	45
ORIENT	39	45
Carlisle	39	45

It seemed as though all the old 'push and run' excellence had returned in the first half against Notts County, and an interval lead of one goal was paltry reward, though it must be admitted that they didn't seem to have a killer instinct for finishing. The second half was somewhat different, County barely mustered up a shot until eight min-

utes from time when a speculative attempt from Masson dipped wickedly and dropped just inside the post, and a fraction under the bar. Yet another point had been lost, after all the one-way traffic of the earlier part. A 4-0 victory by Blackpool over Carlisle added to Orient's worries, though it also diminished Carlisle's chances.

The last Saturday fixtures of the season were vital. Two wins would put O's back in the first division. And so to Saturday 27th April, and the vital matches were: Cardiff v Orient, Sunderland v Blackpool, Carlisle v Aston Villa. The first unlucky blow fell on Orient, as expected. The cool, calm defender, David Payne, broke a leg after a bad tackle but the magnificent O's fought on and Bullock gave them an eighteenth minute lead. It was short lived. Reece equalised four minutes later and there was a ding-dong battle for the winner, but there was to be no further scoring. Then the fans found out that Blackpool had lost 2-1 at Sunder-

Derrick Downing scores—but is ruled offside

land, and Carlisle had beaten Aston Villa 2-0. Carlisle had opposite luck and reports on their match against Villa said they had been fortunate to win, Villa twice hitting the bar.

So it now all rested on the Orient v Aston Villa match to be played on Cup Final eve. There was a rearranged fixture, the original being postponed on 9th February because of a waterlogged pitch. One is left wondering what the outcome would have been if it had been played on its proper date. Orient had to win to go up. Any score would do, as long as it was a win, our goal average being better than Carlisle's. 29,766 turned up at Brisbane Road—if only the club could have relied on this kind of support in earlier seasons. The atmosphere was electric and it was soon obvious that the Orient were very tense. Much of the play was in midfield and the first half was goalless, Orient having slightly more of the play. Then a break on the left wing by Little

put us in trouble. A late tackle by Hoadley sent the winger down in the box, and Graydon scored from the penalty. The writing was on the wall and the O's began to fight. Following a throw in by Roffey, Bullock lobbed in the equaliser. Even though Villa seemed to be playing as if their existence depended on the result, Fairbrother went close. Then came the last chance. From a move on the left by Heppolette and Queen, the ball went to Bullock. His full-blooded, rising drive was tipped over the bar by Cumbes. The 'Super O's', as they had so often been called this campaign, had failed. Just a goal away. Where did they go wrong after the glorious first part of the season? This is impossible to say, but they played too well for too long for it to be explained by saying that it was a flash in the pan, or that the team played above themselves. Once again a factor to be taken into consideration is the number of injuries suffered. When the form started to

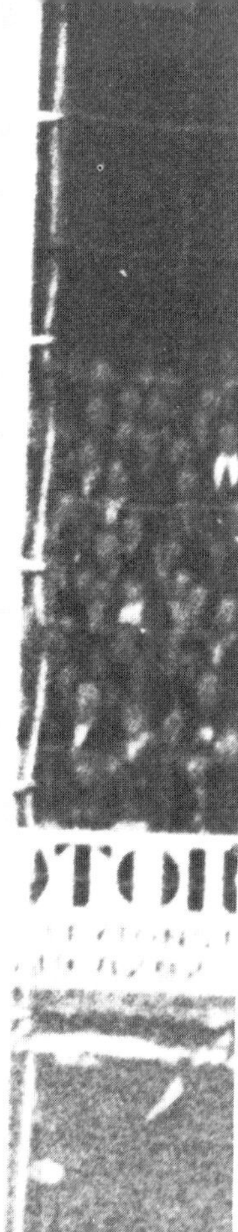

Mickey Bullock scores the O's goal

wane in the New Year, the casualties included Heppolette, Goddard, Jackson, Allen, Downing, Payne, Queen and Bullock, and Roffey went down with appendicitis.

But this was not a season of failure for Orient. One compensation was that they came out top of the *Daily Mail* entertainment League which they had led for almost the entire season. That is something to feel proud of. What a send-off promotion would have been for Arthur Page, whom the club owes so much, for he retires from the Chairmanship and becomes life president this summer, 1974. It is doubtful if any other single person has done so much for the club, with the possible exception of Captain Wells-Holland in the pre-World War One days. Arthur Page personally took up the challenge of finally solving all the club's desperate troubles in 66. What is probably unknown by most of Orient's supporters is that Page, along with another director of the time, Frank Snewin, also pulled the club out of financial trouble in the late 40s.

THE FUTURE

What of the future of the club? Well, the new chairman Mr. Brian Winston, a very successful businessman in his middle thirties, is an ideal choice. He is go-ahead, ambitious, and most important for the Orient, a winner. Many fans will recall his remarks at the meeting in the grandstand in February 73, when he said that he had

Ray Graydon (Villa) scores—dashing Orient's promotion hopes

only met success in all he had undertaken and, on joining the Orient board, stated that he did not contemplate anything other than success in his association with us. This is the spirit the club needs. Max Page, Arthur's son, is also on the board to carry on the family interest, long serving chairman Harry Zussman and Frank Harris making up the team of directors. (Frank Harris's father, George, was a former Orient chairman and was still a member of the board at the time of his death in 49).

There is far more professional outlook in the club now at all levels. What a splendid choice the board made when they appointed George Petchey as manager in 71. Look at the club's progress since that date. He changed the rather defeatist outlook and set about his uphill task quietly and efficiently, the results of which we saw in this wonderful 73/4 season. Petchey's efforts deserved to be rewarded with promotion to the first division. It was not to be this time, but his brand of entertaining and mostly successful soccer will reach that goal, soon. Is there a more loyal and efficient trainer in the land than Peter Angell? This modest ex-QPR player had held the post since October 67, and is invaluable to the club. Physiotherapist Ernie Shepherd is another vital cog in the Orient machinery, especially as we are so unlucky with injuries. Arthur Rowe adds all his experience to the squad as adviser and scout. One of the most satisfying positions must be that of youth team coach, Terry Long. He looks after a

The Champagne stays corked, while Fairbrother and Queen reflect on the nearness of victory

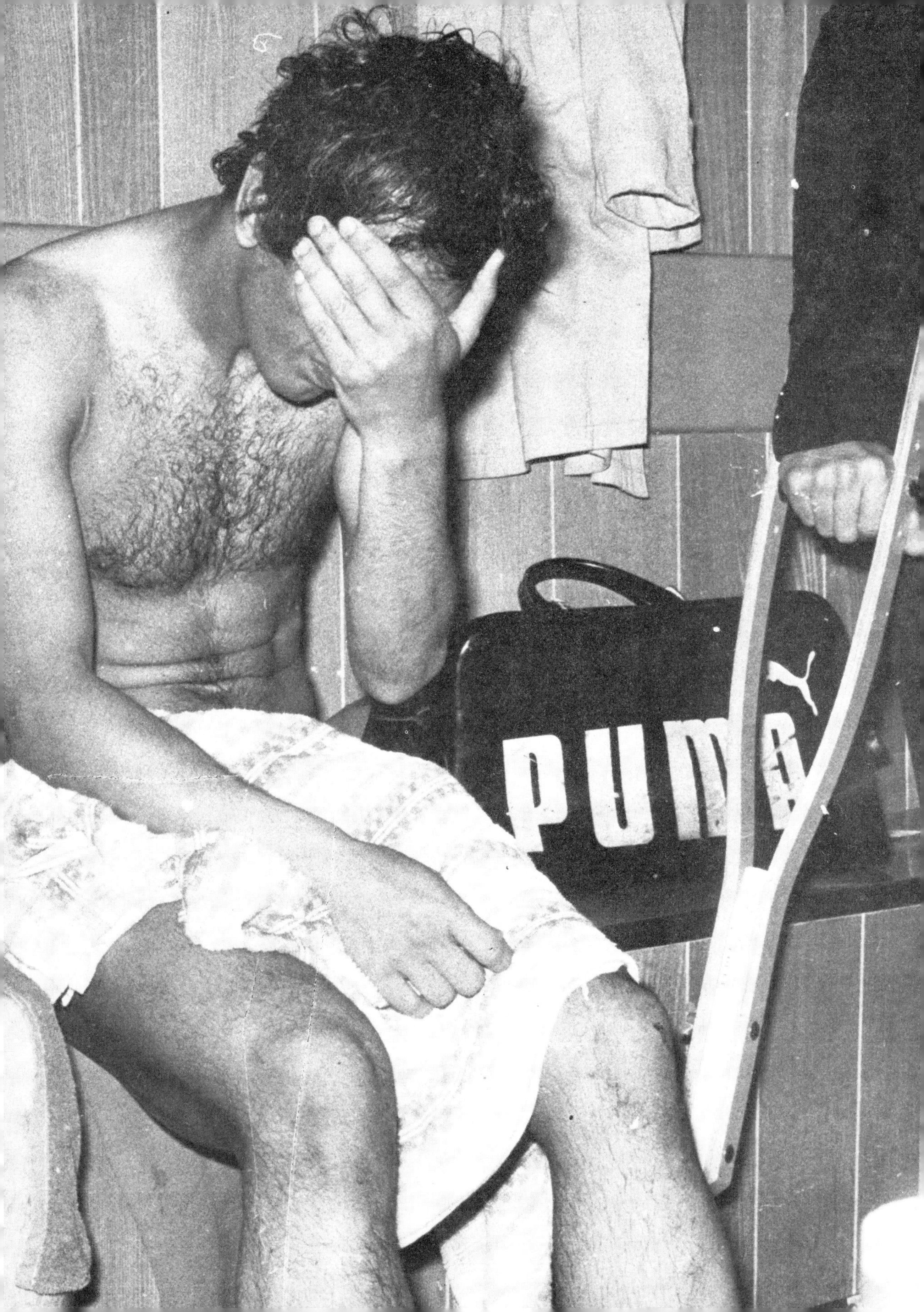
PUMA

real wealth of young talent, like Bobby Fisher, one youngster who has made the first team grade. There are others who must surely follow him into the League side: John Smeulders, Glen Roeder, Cary Hibbs, Nigel Gray, Tony Crealish, Laurie Cunningham, Dean Mooney, Ian Woodward, Bobby Broomfield, Billy Bragg...The list seems endless. Brian Barnes, the club secretary, sees that the administration ticks over smoothly, and perhaps the most under-rated member of the staff is Brian Blower, the commercial manager (and his assistants), who have worked wonders in the pools office during the last few years. This is a very important section of the club; it has grown steadily in recent years.

It is easy to see that the club has never been in such good hands in all departments. Regular membership of the first division is not an impossibility with such an organisation. There was an 82.7 per cent increase in attendance in 73/4 over the previous season, 112,013 more fans. Real Orient fans ride bigger setbacks than just missing promotion. The Orient supporter is made of sterner stuff. So, if you are an Orient fan, whether your initiation came with the saves of Arthur Wood, the power of Frank Neary, the nonchalance of Dave Dunmore, the great headers of Tom Johnston or the guile of Barrie Fairbrother, it's all systems go for 1974/5. There are many unwritten chapters in the history of this fine old club to come yet, so let's enjoy them together. Up the O's!

Captain and journalist Peter Allen▲

The Squad goes off to Spain▼

The Players

GOALKEEPERS

RAY GODDARD. Joined the club early in 1967 having previously been on Fulham's books. A good handler of the ball, he has become a firm favourite with the fans, and has played more matches in goal than any other keeper except Arthur Wood. He made his debut against Workington on 27th May 1967.

JOHN JACKSON. Played over 350 matches for Crystal Palace and represented the FL before coming to us in October 1973. An experienced custodian who was described as one of the best keepers in England in 1972, he made his debut against Luton on 20th October 1973, though sadly hampered by injury in the latter part of the season.

MIKE O'SHAUGHNESSY. As a tall, promising east London schoolboy he signed apprentice forms in 1970, became a full-timer in December 72 and had his first League outing against Hull City on 6th October 1973.

JOHN SMEULDERS. Still young enough to play in the Colts he became an apprentice in 1972 and, seen to be very promising, joined the full-time staff in 74.

DEFENDERS

DAVID PAYNE. A cool, calm full back, capable of playing in midfield too, he signed on after 9 years and 300 appearances for Palace, where he was picked for the England Under 23 team in 68. He made his Orient debut on 25th August 73 against Sunderland. In April 74 he broke his leg in a match at Cardiff.

BILL ROFFEY. Only twenty, an enthusiastic defender with attacking flare, he played for Palace in the first division before signing on in October 73 and playing his opening game against Preston North End on 3rd November.

DERRICK DOWNING. He made nearly 200 appearances for Middlesborough before coming here in May 1972 and having his first game against Oxford United on 12th August of that year. He is a versatile and adroit player and, though previously a winger or midfield man, he has been mainly in the defence this season.

PETER BENNETT. The man who took over the captaincy when Mancini left, this former West Ham player and youth international came to Orient in October 1970 and first turned out against Sheffield Wednesday on 19th of that month. A serious groin injury in March 73 has kept him out of the side for a long period and he has made only two outings this season.

TOM WALLEY. A former Welsh Under 23 and a full Welsh international in his days at Watford, he played for Arsenal and joined Orient in December 71, making his debut against Swindon on 12th of that month. Playing either in the back four or midfield, he specialises in long accurate passes. He had an excellent season in 73/4.

PHIL HOADLEY. A former youth cap, he also came from Palace, and made his debut against Blackpool on 9th October 71. For two seasons now he has been ever present in the side. He has a powerful shot and was switched from right-back to centre-half (centre-back) for the 73/4 season.

IAN WOODWARD. Previously with Coventry youth team, he is a sturdy defender who came as an apprentice in 71 and signed on

Some players' wives (l. to r): Mrs Queen, Mrs Payne, Mrs Allen, Mrs Fairbrother, Mrs Jackson, Mrs Goddard, Mrs Hoadley and Mrs Brisley

full-time in December 72.

MALCOLM LINTON. A strong, quick tackler, clearing his lines, he was a Southend amateur before coming here in the summer of 72. He made his debut against Portsmouth on 23rd December 72 and did well in the latter stages of that season.

PAUL HARRIS. A tall, strong, central defender, good in the air, he had an excellent season in 71/2. From a Waltham Forest schools player he came through the Orient youth team, joining in 69 as an apprentice, and signing professional forms in 1970. He made his debut against Cardiff City on 1st May 71.

NIGEL GRAY. A tall, promising centre-half, he joined as an apprentice in 73 and full-time in 74. He has had experience with the reserves but has yet to make a League appearance.

MIDFIELD

JOHN BOYLE. A midfield player who can also turn out as full back, this experienced Scot played over 200 games for Chelsea before making his Orient debut against Swindon on 22nd December 73.

TERRY BRISLEY. Small, but energetic and very hard-working, he was with us as a schoolboy before becoming an apprentice in 66 and a full-timer in 68. He came in as a substitute against Carlisle on 5th September 70, having his first game, against Bolton on 9th January 71.

PETER ALLEN. Captain of Orient this season, Peter is a shrewd and clever forager. Only two players have had more League games for us, Arthur Wood and Stan Charlton. From the Spurs youth team he came here for a short spell as an amateur and then signed professional forms in summer 65. He made his debut in the League Cup against Coventry on 22nd September 65, and had his first League game against Portsmouth on 25th September.

TONY GREALISH. This Irish lad is small in stature but has enough talent to reach the top, and can play full back as well as midfield. He was an apprentice from 72 until early 74, when he signed on as a professional.

GARY HIBBS. Voted the best young player of 73/4 he joined Orient as an apprentice in 72 and signed full-time in 74. Surely he will turn out for the League side very soon.

GLEN ROEDER. Stylish Glen came to us as an apprentice in 72 after being with Arsenal on amateur terms. He became a full-time professional during 73/4.

BOBBY BROOMFIELD. A tall midfield player who can play in attack, he joined as an apprentice in 73 after experience with West Ham.

RICKY HEPPOLETTE. This very clever and talented performer, a favourite with the fans, is an Anglo-Indian who came to us for a big fee having played about 150 games for Preston North End. He made his debut against QPR on 23rd December 72.

BOBBY FISHER. Recommended to the club by Mark Lazarus, he signed as an apprentice in 71 and became a full-timer in 73. This lad has class, reads a game very well, and can play full back as well as in midfield. He came on as substiture against Sunderland on 25th August 73, and had his first match, against Bolton, on 9th September.

FORWARDS

BILLY BRAGG. A live wire striker who was apprenticed in 72 and joined the full-time staff at the close of the 73/4 term.

MICKEY BULLOCK. A cool, clever type who specialises in laying the ball off with his head and keeps the attack moving with intelligent flicks. Top scorer in the 69/70 promotion team, he had an aggregate of 65 League and Cup goals for Orient at the close of the 73/4 season. An ex-schoolboy international, his first club was Birmingham City. He came to us from Oxford United and made his debut against Hartlepool on 26th October 68.

GERRY QUEEN. Scotsman Gerry had experience with St. Mirren and Kilmarnock before moving, first to Palace, and then to Orient in September 72 for a large fee. He made his debut on the 23rd of that month against QPR. Difficult to contain in his best form, he is our number one penalty taker.

BARRIE FAIRBROTHER. Voted player of the year by the fans, this real hard grafter came up through Orient's youth teams after a short spell with Spurs juniors. He was the most prolific goalscorer ever for the Colts, was apprenticed in 67 and became a professional in 68. He made his debut against Mansfield on 30th August 68 and scored the only goal of the match.

DEAN MOONEY. Tall, blond Dean, nicknamed 'Dixie' for obvious reasons, scored many youth and reserve goals and is now a good prospect. He was apprenticed in 72 and signed on full-time for the 73/4 season.

LAURIE CUNNINGHAM. Another talent soon for the first team, he is a fast and tricky winger, apprenticed in 72 and becoming a full-timer in 74.

IAN FILBY. Similar in style to Fairbrother, this go-for-goal striker has been a good scorer for the reserves. He was apprenticed in 70 and became full-time in 72.

The Pools Office

Brian Blower

ORIENT POOLS STAFF

The Staff of Orient Pools are a group of workers who help to raise funds for the Club from its Weekly "Bingo" Tickets and various Draws throughout the year, as well as running the Sportsmans Club and all of its activities. All of these activities come under the wing of Brian Blower, Commercial Manager, who has now been with the Club for 9 years taking over the activities from Orient Ex-Player, Johnny Heartburn who is now doing a similar job for Fulham. The Pools Office work as a team. Looking after the General administration of the Office is Rosemary Brines who joined the Club 7 years ago and really enjoys her work because of the variety, then comes Pools Representative Sandra Callaghan who joined the Club 4 years ago and travels some 500 miles each week calling on many of the Pools Agents.

Brian says: "Things have really changed since I came to the Club. I remember the time that they went round with the bucket to help raise money. I think that this was the turning point in the Club's history. Everybody connected with the Club, including the Directors, did everything possible to save this Club from folding up. A new approach to the running of the Club was taken and look how it succeeded. Last season we were only just pipped for promotion and I am sure with the set-up as it is now it won't be too long before we end up in the First Division. I think that our Supporters deserve this break as well as the Club. In my time at the Orient I can remember working with Les Gore, Dick Graham, Jimmy Bloomfield and now George Petchey. For the benefit of our Supporters we now operate the Sportsmans Club. This superseded the old Supporters Section and I feel the advantages of being a member of the Sportsmans Club are fantastic. Functions are arranged at our Springhill Club almost weekly, also all the away travel, dinners and many other different things are arranged for our Supporters. All it costs to be a member is £1 per year. This now takes a lot of my time and the Pools Office staff's, but we think it's time well spent. I came to work for the Orient when I saw an article in the paper about the Club and advertising for an assistant to Johnny Heartburn. I applied for the job and was told if I could earn my first week's wages I could have the job. I have been here 9 years now so I should think that I did that. I had only seen the Orient play twice before coming to work for them. I think that this was an advantage in my work; I can truly say I was not an Orient supporter. This was put right after working for the Club for a few weeks. It is catching I think that everybody who comes to the Orient must support them; they grow on you. The people who help us to raise money are our Pools Agents and like our supporters are the best in the country. Both the Club and I personally would like to thank them for all their help."

Afterword

THE FUTURE OF ORIENT

After I had spent eight years at West Ham as an amateur and then professional footballer, and then moving on to Queens Park Rangers for another eight year spell, I moved to Crystal Palace. Arthur Rowe had just taken over as manager of Palace, and looking round the ground and talking with him we were both agreed Palace would be in the First Division within ten years.

As you know, Palace reached the First Division in the tenth year. During that period of years, after five years as a player, I had become Youth Manager, then after a year, I was promoted to First Team Coach. I worked under three managers at Palace as team Coach, and each in his own way added something to my own way of doing things. Once we arrived in the First Division, it then made me more determined to go on my own. After two years in the First Division the offer came to come to the Orient. Having turned down several offers to other Clubs, it was a great wrench to leave Palace. I had been with them for twelve years and in that time they had risen from the Fourth Division to hold their position in the First. My family had made lots of friends there, but if I was going to leave, this was the time.

So we arrived at Orient. The Club had survived one year in the Second Division and we needed to restaff; as well as good facilities, a training ground was a priority. Also the Club had to sell a player before we could buy. As you now know, we sold three or four players and bought three or four.

The lucky part of most of our buying was that Palace were in the throes of selling cheaply some of their best players: Hoadley, 19 years of age, Roffey, 19, Payne, 24, were examples. Also we were lucky to be able to buy Heppolette, Walley and Downing to establish the Club in the Second Division. With the added players Queen and Jackson, we nearly won a place in the First Division and finished top of the *Daily Mail* entertainment league. We had also built up the reserves with players whose average age was 19 years old. Also our Juniors have been built up into one of the best youth sides in London, finishing second in the Eastern Counties League and winning the London Youth Cup.

So, after three years, we have now established the Club well in the Second Division. The future looks very bright for the Club, for we have improved the Orient no end, with new dressing rooms, and a players room where the wives can wait before and after the game. We have also found probably the best training ground in London; a Sportsmens Club at the ground where members can enjoy the facilities of the Club, and the Vice Presidents have their own exclusive Club.

We have a new office section and a new secretary. Also the football staff have been built up into a good team off the field: Peter Angell has the trainers duties, Terry Long coaches the reserves and apprentices, and Ernie Shepherd, the Club physio has just taken over the duties as physio to the Indian Cricket touring team.

Behind the scenes we have Arthur Rowe, organising our scouting along with several local managers, among them Mr. Newman of Beaumont from whose team we have taken seven players; five have turned professional with us.

We have now excellent Press facilities, a Press room and Box.

Many improvements have been made to the ground; seats have replaced forms in the stand. This year toilets have been rebuilt and more bars have been placed around the ground. The ground itself has been improved with a new drainage system and the seeding has been done by seeding specialists for the last two years.

The priority now is success! The players have tasted success up to a point and are thirsting for more. Everything has been improved and with the help of the Chairman and the Board we will now go all out to become a First Division Club.

The real future is with our young players. One day we hope to produce a team who are all our own players who have come through from our youth teams.

This is our ideal and perhaps in the near future you will see it happen.

The Club now has a high reputation for good football and clean football. This will stay. We hope that our supporters will have patience with us and encourage us to go on and achieve all our dreams and promotion to Division One.

George Petchey

Statistics

ORIENT'S RECORD AGAINST EACH LEAGUE CLUB
Orient's record shown first (abandoned matches not included).

Season	Div.	H.	A
ALDERSHOT			
32/3	3s	2-3	0-4
33/4	3s	9-2	0-0
34/5	3s	3-1	1-1
35/6	3s	0-1	0-1
36/7	3s	1-1	1-1
37/8	3s	2-1	2-1
38/9	3s	2-0	0-1
46/7	3s	1-3	0-0
47/8	3s	o-3	0-0
48/9	3s	1-2	1-1
49/50	3s	2-7	0-2
50/1	3s	1-0	1-3
51/2	3s	0-1	1-0
52/3	3s	4-1	0-2
53/4	3s	1-2	1-1
54/5	3s	1-5	1-0
55/6	3s	8-3	1-1
FA Cup			
32/3	R1	0-1	
35/6	R1	0-0	1-0
ARSENAL			
13/4	2	1-0	2-2
14/5	2	1-0	1-2
62/3	1	1-2	0-2
FA Cup			
10/1	R1	1-2	
51/2	R5	0-3	
71/2	R6	0-1	
ASTON VILLA			
59/60	2	0-0	0-1
62/3	1	0-2	0-1
72/3	2	4-0	0-1
73/4	2	1-1	2-2
FA Cup			
28/9	R4	0-8	0-0
BARNSLEY			
05/6	2	0-0	1-4
06/7	2	1-0	2-3
07/8	2	2-0	2-2
08/9	2	1-1	0-3
09/10	2	4-0	1-2
10/1	2	3-0	2-1
11/2	2	2-0	1-2
12/3	2	2-2	0-0
13/4	2	1-0	1-2
14/5	2	4-2	0-1
19/20	2	2-0	1-2
20/1	2	3-2	0-1
21/2	2	2-1	0-4
22/3	2	0-1	1-2
23/4	2	2-1	0-1
24/5	2	0-0	1-1
25/6	2	4-0	1-3
26/7	2	0-1	2-4
27/8	2	2-0	2-4
28/9	2	3-1	0-2
56/7	2	2-0	0-3
57/8	2	2-1	0-3
58/9	2	5-1	3-1
68/9	3	1-1	2-2
69/70	3	4-2	2-1
League Cup			
64/5	R2	3-0	
BARROW			
67/8	3	4-2	0-1
68/9	3	1-2	1-3
69/70	3	2-0	1-1
BIRMINGHAM CITY			
08/9	2	3-2	0-1
09/10	2	3-0	2-1
10/1	2	2-1	1-0
11/2	2	2-0	0-4
12/3	2	0-2	1-1
13/4	2	2-2	0-2
14/5	2	1-1	0-1
19/20	2	2-1	1-2
20/1	2	1-1	0-0
62/3	1	2-2	2-2
65/6	2	2-1	2-2
70/1	2	0-2	0-1
71/2	2	0-1	0-2
FA Cup			
51/2	R4		1-0
55/6	R4	0-4	
67/8	R4		0-3
BLACKBURN ROVERS			
56/7	2	1-1	3-3
57/8	2	5-1	1-4
62/3	1	1-1	1-1
70/1	2	1-1	0-0
FA Cup			
58/9	R3		2-4
League Cup			
73/4	R2	2-0	
BLACKPOOL			
05/6	2	0-0	0-3
06/7	2	0-0	3-1
07/8	2	1-1	0-5
08/9	2	1-1	3-1
9/10	2	2-1	2-2
10/1	2	2-1	1-1
11/2	2	2-0	0-1
12/3	2	1-0	0-2
13/4	2	2-0	0-0
14/5	2	2-0	1-5
19/20	2	3-0	0-3
20/1	2	0-0	2-2
21/2	2	3-0	0-2
22/3	2	0-1	0-0
23/4	2	1-0	0-3
24/5	2	1-0	0-1
25/6	2	2-2	0-3
26/7	2	1-0	0-6
27/8	2	2-5	1-0
28/9	2	2-4	1-0
62/3	1	0-2	2-3
71/2	2	0-1	1-4
72/3	2	2-0	1-1
73/4	2	3-2	1-1
League Cup			
61/2	R2	1-1	1-5
BOLTON WANDERERS			
08/9	2	0-2	0-2
10/11	2	0-0	0-2
62/3	1	0-1	1-0
64/5	2	3-1	0-0
65/6	2	1-0	0-2
70/1	2	3-1	1-0
73/4	2	3-0	1-1
BOURNEMOUTH			
29/30	3s	0-0	1-5

Barrie Fairbrother, Orient Player of the Year collects his trophy

30/1	3s	0-0	1-1
31/2	3s	1-2	1-0
32/3	3s	1-1	2-4
33/4	3s	4-1	0-2
34/5	3s	0-1	0-1
35/6	3s	1-1	0-2
36/7	3s	2-1	1-2
37/8	3s	3-0	1-2
38/9	3s	1-1	0-0
46/7	3s	2-3	0-2
47/8	3s	2-0	1-1
48/9	3s	1-2	0-3
49/50	3s	2-1	1-4
50/1	3s	2-0	0-5
51/2	3s	1-0	2-3
52/3	3s	2-2	1-4
53/4	3s	5-0	2-1
54/5	3s	3-1	3-0
55/6	3s	3-0	1-3
66/7	3	1-0	0-1
67/8	3	1-0	0-0
68/9	3	1-0	1-0
69/70	3	3-0	2-0

FA Cup

73/4	R3	2-1	

BRADFORD P.A.

08/9	2	2-0	1-0
09/10	2	1-0	1-3
10/1	2	1-0	0-3
11/2	2	2-0	1-2
12/3	2	1-0	0-3
13/4	2	1-0	0-1
21/2	2	1-0	1-3
28/9	2	1-0	1-2

FA Cup

20/1	R1		0-1

BRADFORD CITY

05/6	2	4-2	0-3
06/7	2	1-1	2-5
07/8	2	0-3	0-1
22/3	2	1-0	2-1
23/4	2	1-1	0-0
24/5	2	0-0	0-0
25/6	2	3-1	3-0
26/7	2	1-1	3-1
69/70	3	2-1	1-0

BRENTFORD

29/30	3s	1-1	1-3
30/1	3s	3-0	0-3
31/2	3s	2-2	0-3
32/3	3s	1-5	2-4
54/5	3s	0-1	0-2
55/6	3s	2-1	0-1

FA Cup

55/6	R2	4-1	
61/2	R3	2-1	1-1
66/7	R2	0-0	1-3

League Cup

73/4	R1		2-1

BRIGHTON & HOVE

29/30	3s	4-1	0-1
30/1	3s	1-0	1-3
31/2	3s	2-2	1-1
32/3	3s	2-0	0-0
33/4	3s	2-1	0-0
34/5	3s	6-0	0-3
35/6	3s	6-0	0-3
36/7	3s	2-0	1-1
37/8	3s	0-3	1-2
38/9	3s	2-0	0-2
46/7	3s	2-1	1-2
47/8	3s	2-1	0-0
48/9	3s	0-3	1-3
49/50	3s	0-1	2-2
50/1	3s	2-1	0-3
51/2	3s	2-1	1-3
52/3	3s	3-0	1-3
53/4	3s	0-2	1-2
54/5	3s	0-0	1-2
54/5	3s	0-0	0-1
55/6	3s	0-1	1-1
58/9	2	2-2	2-2
59/60	2	3-2	1-1
60/61	2	2-1	1-1
61/2	2	4-1	1-1
66/7	3	1-0	0-1
67/8	3	1-2	1-1
68/9	3	3-2	0-2
69/70	3	1-1	0-0
72/3	2	1-0	1-2

FA Cup

13	R2		1-3

League Cup

66/7	R1		0-1

BRISTOL CITY

05/6	2	0-2	0-1
11/12	2	4-0	0-1
12/13	2	0-0	0-1
13/14	2	5-2	0-3
14/15	2	2-0	0-3
19/20	2	1-0	1-1
20/1	2	0-0	0-2
21/2	2	0-1	1-2
23/4	2	2-0	2-0
27/8	2	4-2	0-1
28/9	2	0-1	0-1
32/3	3s	2-2	0-3
33/4	3s	4-0	0-3
34/5	3s	4-0	0-0
35/6	3s	2-0	0-2
36/7	3s	0-0	0-4
37/8	3s	0-0	0-2
38/9	3s	1-1	1-3
46/7	3s	4-1	0-3
47/8	3s	0-2	1-6
48/9	3s	3-1	0-3
49/50	3s	1-0	0-0

50/1	3s	0-2	1-4
51/2	3s	0-2	1-4
52/3	3s	1-3	1-2
53/4	3s	4-1	0-1
54/5	3s	4-1	0-5
56/7	2	2-2	2-4
57/8	2	4-0	2-2
58/9	2	4-2	1-0
59/60	2	3-1	1-1
65/6	2	3-1	1-1
70/1	2	1-1	0-0
71/2	2	2-0	3-5
72/3	2	0-2	2-2
73/4	2	0-1	2-0

BRISTOL ROVERS

29/30	3s	3-0	0-0
30/1	3s	3-1	1-4
31/2	3s	1-0	1-2
32/3	3s	0-3	0-2
33/4	3s	0-3	0-2
34/5	3s	5-2	2-1
35/6	3s	2-0	1-1
36/7	3s	2-1	0-4
37/8	3s	1-0	2-3
38/9	3s	2-1	0-1
46/7	3s	3-0	1-6
47/8	3s	2-4	2-0
48/9	3s	1-1	3-2
49/50	3s	1-0	0-3
50/1	3s	1-0	1-2
51/2	3s	3-3	0-1
52/3	3s	3-3	1-2
56/7	2	1-3	0-4
58/9	2	1-3	3-1
59/60	2	3-2	2-3
60/1	2	3-2	2-4
61/2	2	2-3	1-2
66/7	3	0-2	0-1
67/8	3	2-2	2-0
68/9	3	2-1	1-0
69/70	3	0-0	0-1

FA Cup

29/30	R3	1-0	
52/3	R1	1-1	0-1

BURNLEY

05/6	2	3-0	0-3
06/7	2	2-1	0-3
07/8	2	0-1	0-3
08/9	2	0-1	1-0
09/10	2	2-1	0-2
10/1	2	0-2	0-2
11/2	2	1-2	0-1
12/3	2	2-0	0-5
62/3	1	0-1	0-2
71/2	2	1-0	1-6
72/3	2	1-1	2-1

FA Cup

61/2	R4	0-1	1-1

BURTON UNITED

05/6	2	0-1	0-1
06/7	2	1-0	1-2

BURY

12/13	2	1-2	0-0
13/14	2	1-0	0-0
14/15	2	2-2	0-3
19/20	2	2-1	0-3
20/1	2	1-0	1-0
21/2	2	3-1	0-0
22/3	2	0-2	1-5
23/4	2	1-0	0-0
56/7	2	4-3	3-1
61/2	2	2-0	1-0
63/4	2	1-1	2-1
64/5	2	1-0	1-2
65/6	2	2-2	0-3
67/8	3	1-0	0-1
69/70	3	3-0	1-0

FA Cup

67/8	R3	1-0	

League Cup

62/3	R5	0-2	

CARDIFF CITY

20/1	2	2-0	0-0
31/2	3s	1-1	1-5
32/3	3s	3-0	1-6
33/4	3s	4-2	2-1
34/5	3s	0-1	0-3
35/6	3s	2-1	1-4
36/7	3s	0-1	1-2
37/8	3s	1-1	0-2
38/9	3s	1-1	2-1
46/7	3s	0-1	0-1
57/8	2	4-2	1-1
58/9	2	3-0	1-2
59/60	2	3-4	1-5
63/4	2	4-0	1-2
64/5	2	1-3	2-0
65/6	2	1-1	1-3
70/1	2	0-0	0-1
71/2	2	4-1	0-1
72/3	2	0-0	1-3
73/4	2	1-2	1-1

FA Cup

31/2	R2		0-4
57/8	R4		1-4

CARLISLE UNITED

65/6	2	2-1	0-1
70/1	2	1-1	0-2
71/2	2	2-1	0-2
72/3	2	2-1	0-1
73/4	2	0-1	0-3

FA Cup

36/7	R2		1-4

CHARLTON ATHLETIC

33/4	3s	1-3	1-1
34/5	3s	1-2	1-2
57/8	2	3-2	2-3
58/9	2	6-1	1-4
59/60	2	2-0	0-0
60/1	2	1-1	0-2
61/2	2	2-0	2-1
63/4	2	0-3	2-1
64/5	2	4-2	0-2
65/6	2	1-2	0-3
70/1	2	0-0	0-2
71/2	2	3-2	2-1

FA Cup

35/6	R3	3-0	

League Cup

62/3	R4	3-2	
64/5	R3		1-2

CHELSEA

05/6	2	0-3	1-6
06/7	2	0-1	1-2
10/1	2	0-0	0-1
11/2	2	1-4	0-3
24/5	2	0-0	1-1
25/6	2	1-2	3-1
26/7	2	3-0	1-2
27/8	2	2-1	0-1
28/9	2	1-0	2-2

FA Cup

56/7	R3	0-2	
71/2	R5	3-2	

CHESTER

FA Cup

34/5	R2	1-3	

League Cup

60/1	R1	1-0	2-2
62/3	R3	9-2	

CHESTERFIELD

05/6	2	3-3	1-1
06/7	2	1-2	1-2
07/8	2	5-1	1-1
08/9	2	1-1	0-2

FA Cup

05/6	R1	0-0	0-3
25/6	R3		1-0

League Cup

60/1	R2	0-1	

COLCHESTER UNITED

50/1	3s	1-1	0-1
51/2	3s	7-0	1-0
52/3	3s	5-3	1-3
53/4	3s	3-1	0-1
54/5	3s	2-0	2-2
55/6	3s	6-0	1-2

COVENTRY CITY

66/7	3	3-3	2-2
67/8	3	1-1	1-1

19/20	2	2-2	0-0
20/1	2	0-0	1-1
21/2	2	4-0	2-1
22/3	2	0-0	1-2
23/4	2	4-0	1-1
24/5	2	1-2	0-1
29/30	3s	3-1	2-5
30/1	3s	3-3	0-4
31/2	3s	5-2	2-4
32/3	3s	2-1	0-5
33/4	3s	0-0	1-3
34/5	3s	0-1	0-4
35/6	3s	0-1	0-2
52/3	3s	1-2	0-3
53/4	3s	1-0	0-4
54/5	3s	1-0	2-2
55/6	3s	3-1	0-3
64/5	2	1-3	1-1
65/6	2	1-1	1-1

FA Cup

31/2	R1	2-0	2-2
72/3	R3	1-4	

League Cup

65/6	R2	0-3	

CREWE ALEXANDRA

68/9	3	2-0	0-2

CRYSTAL PALACE

21/2	2	0-0	0-1
22/3	2	3-1	0-2
23/4	2	1-0	1-2
24/5	2	3-0	1-0
29/30	3s	2-1	0-3
30/1	3s	2-1	0-3
31/2	3s	1-3	0-0
32/3	3s	4-1	1-2
33/4	3s	2-0	2-3
34/5	3s	2-0	0-1
35/6	3s	1-0	2-2
36/7	3s	1-1	3-2
37/8	3s	0-2	0-1
38/9	3s	0-2	0-1
46/7	3s	0-1	0-2
47/8	3s	0-1	0-2
48/9	3s	1-1	0-2
49/50	3s	2-2	1-1
50/1	3s	2-0	1-1
51/2	3s	0-4	1-2
52/3	3s	0-0	2-2
53/4	3s	2-0	2-2
54/5	3s	2-1	1-1
55/6	3s	8-0	2-1
64/5	2	0-1	0-1
65/6	2	0-2	1-2
73/4	2	3-0	0-0

League Cup

68/9	R3	0-1	

DARLINGTON

25/6	2	1-2	0-6
26/7	2	0-4	1-2
66/7	3	1-2	0-0

FA Cup

48/9	R2		0-1

DERBY COUNTY

07/8	2	1-0	0-4
08/9	2	2-0	0-1
09/10	2	0-2	0-1
10/1	2	1-0	1-3
11/2	2	3-0	1-5
14/5	2	0-1	3-0
21/2	2	3-2	0-3
22/3	2	0-0	0-0
23/4	2	2-0	0-1
24/5	2	0-1	0-3
25/6	2	0-1	0-3
57/8	2	1-1	0-2
58/9	2	1-1	0-2
59/60	2	3-0	1-1
60/1	2	2-1	1-3
61/2	2	2-0	2-1
63/4	2	3-0	0-1
64/5	2	1-4	0-1
65/6	2	0-0	3-1

FA Cup

62/3	R4	3-0	

DONCASTER ROVERS

56/7	2	1-1	1-6
57/8	2	2-0	0-2
66/7	3	4-1	2-2

FA Cup

53/4	R5	3-1	

EVERTON

62/3	1	3-0	0-3

FA Cup

11/2	R1	1-2	
51/2	R2	0-0	3-1

EXETER CITY

29/30	3s	3-0	0-4
30/1	3s	2-3	1-6
31/2	3s	2-2	3-4
32/3	3s	2-2	0-3
33/4	3s	4-0	3-0
34/5	3s	0-3	1-1
35/6	3s	1-2	3-2
36/7	3s	1-0	2-0
37/8	3s	2-1	0-2
38/9	3s	3-3	1-2
	3s	3-1	1-3
46/7	3s	2-4	1-1
47/8	3s	5-2	1-3
48/9	3s	4-1	1-1
49/50	3s	1-3	0-0
51/2	3s	3-0	1-6

52/3	3s	2-0	1-0
53/4	3s	3-1	1-2
54/5	3s	5-0	7-1
55/6	3s	1-1	1-1

FULHAM

07/8	2	0-1	0-4
08/9	2	1-1	2-1
09/10	2	0-0	0-0
10/1	2	1-0	1-1
11/2	2	4-0	2-0
12/3	2	2-1	1-1
13/4	2	1-0	0-2
14/5	2	2-1	0-4
19/20	2	0-1	1-2
20/1	2	3-0	0-1
21/2	2	4-2	0-2
22/3	2	0-2	0-0
23/4	2	0-0	0-0
24/5	2	3-0	2-0
25/6	2	1-1	2-0
26/7	2	2-3	0-2
27/8	2	3-2	0-2
29/30	3s	2-4	2-2
30/1	3s	2-0	0-2
31/2	3s	0-1	1-5
56/7	2	0-2	1-3
57/8	2	1-3	1-3
58/9	2	0-2	2-5
62/3	1	1-1	2-0
69/70	3	3-1	1-1
71/2	2	1-0	1-2
72/3	2	3-2	1-1
73/4	2	1-0	3-0

FA Cup

53/4	R4	2-1	

League Cup

68/9	R2	1-0	
69/70	R1	0-0	1-3
70/1	R1		0-1

GAINSBOROUGH TRINITY

05/6	2	1-0	1-2
06/7	2	3-1	1-3
07/8	2	2-0	0-0
08/9	2	2-2	0-2
09/10	2	2-0	1-0
10/1	2	1-0	1-3
11/2	2	3-0	2-0

GATESHEAD

(Played against Orient only under their former name of South Shields)

19/20	2	4-0	0-2
20/1	2	1-0	0-3
21/2	2	0-1	1-1
22/3	2	3-0	1-1
23/4	2	3-0	1-1
24/5	2	0-0	0-2
25/6	2	1-2	0-1
26/7	2	1-0	1-2
27/8	2	2-2	2-2

GILLINGHAM

29/30	3s	2-0	0-2
30/1	3s	0-2	0-0
31/2	3s	3-1	2-0
32/3	3s	1-2	1-3
33/4	3s	2-1	1-1
34/5	3s	2-2	0-1
35/6	3s	3-1	0-3
36/7	3s	2-0	2-0
37/8	3s	3-0	2-1
50/1	3s	4-0	0-1
51/2	3s	1-0	1-1
52/3	3s	1-1	2-3
53/4	3s	3-1	2-1
54/5	3s	2-2	0-0
55/6	3s	2-0	1-0
66/7	3	0-1	0-0
67/8	3	0-4	3-2
68/9	3	1-1	2-2
69/70	3	1-2	1-0

FA Cup

47/8	R1		0-1
60/1	R3		6-2
68/9	R1	1-1	1-2

League Cup

67/8	R1	1-3	
68/9	R1	3-0	2-2

GLOSSOP NORTH END

05/6	2	2-0	0-5
06/7	2	3-0	0-3
07/8	2	0-0	1-2
08/9	2	0-0	1-2
09/10	2	0-0	1-3
10/1	2	4-0	3-1
11/2	2	2-1	3-3
12/3	2	1-0	0-3
13/4	2	5-1	3-0
14/5	2	5-2	1-3

GRIMSBY TOWN

05/6	2	1-2	1-4
06/7	2	1-0	2-1
07/8	2	2-1	0-0
08/9	2	2-1	0-1
09/10	2	0-0	0-2
11/2	2	1-0	1-2
12/3	2	1-2	2-1
13/4	2	0-0	0-2
14/5	2	2-1	1-2
19/20	2	3-0	0-2
26/7	2	2-4	2-2
27/8	2	1-2	2-2
28/9	2	3-1	1-6
56/7	2	1-1	0-0
57/8	2	5-1	2-7
58/9	2	0-1	1-4
63/4	2	0-0	1-1
66/7	3	1-1	2-1
67/8	3	1-0	0-0

FA Cup

1933/4	R3		0-1

HALIFAX TOWN

Season	Div	Home	Away
1969/70	3	1-0	1-1

HARTLEPOOL

Season	Div	Home	Away
68/9	3	0-1	0-0

HUDDERSFIELD TOWN

Season	Div	Home	Away
10/11	2	2-0	0-2
11/12	2	2-1	0-0
12/13	2	1-1	0-0
13/14	2	0-0	0-1
14/5	2	3-1	1-1
19/20	2	0-1	1-2
56/7	2	3-1	0-3
57/8	2	3-1	0-2
58/9	2	2-5	0-0
59/60	2	2-1	1-1
60/1	2	2-0	0-1
61/2	2	3-0	1-1
63/4	2	2-3	1-2
64/5	2	1-0	0-0
65/6	2	0-2	1-1
72/3	2	3-1	1-1

HULL CITY

Season	Div	Home	Away
05/6	2	0-1	1-3
06/7	2	2-1	0-2
07/8	2	1-0	0-5
08/9	2	0-0	0-3
09/10	2	0-0	0-3
10/1	2	1-1	2-1
11/2	2	4-0	2-0
12/3	2	2-1	1-2
13/4	2	3-0	0-2
14/5	2	3-0	0-2
19/20	2	2-2	1-3
20/1	2	1-1	0-3
21/2	2	1-1	0-3
22/3	2	2-0	1-2
23/4	2	0-0	2-2
24/5	2	0-0	1-2
25/6	2	0-0	0-2
26/7	2	1-2	0-4
27/8	2	0-0	2-2
28/9	2	0-2	0-0
59/60	2	3-1	2-1
70/1	2	0-1	2-5
71/2	2	1-0	1-1
72/3	2	0-0	0-2
73/4	2	1-1	1-1

FA Cup

Season	Rd	Home	Away
62/3	R3	1-1	2-0

IPSWICH TOWN

Season	Div	Home	Away
38/9	3s	1-1	0-3
46/7	3s	2-2	0-0
47/8	3s	1-1	0-1
48/9	3s	1-1	2-2
49/50	3s	4-0	4-4
50/1	3s	2-0	2-2
51/2	3s	2-0	0-1
52/3	3s	3-1	1-0
53/4	3s	1-2	1-3
55/6	3s	1-2	0-2
57/8	2	2-0	3-5
58/9	2	2-0	1-2
59/60	2	4-1	3-6
60/1	2	1-3	2-6
62/3	1	1-2	1-1
64/5	2	0-0	1-1
65/6	2	1-4	2-3

FA Cup

Season	Rd	Home	Away
50/1	R1	1-2	

LEEDS UNITED

Season	Div	Home	Away
05/6	2	0-0	1-6
06/7	2	1-1	2-3
07/8	2	0-0	2-5
08/9	2	0-0	0-0
09/10	2	0-2	1-2
10/1	2	1-0	0-1
11/2	2	2-1	2-0
12/3	2	2-0	1-3
13/4	2	3-1	0-0
14/5	2	2-0	1-0
20/1	2	1-0	1-2
21/2	2	4-2	0-2
22/3	2	3-0	0-0
23/4	2	0-1	0-1
27/8	2	2-1	0-4
60/1	2	0-1	3-1
61/2	2	0-0	0-0
63/4	2	0-2	1-2

LEICESTER CITY

Season	Div	Home	Away
05/6	2	0-2	1-2
06/7	2	1-0	1-2
07/8	2	0-1	2-0
09/10	2	3-0	0-4
10/1	2	3-1	1-2
11/2	2	4-1	0-2
12/3	2	1-1	0-1
13/4	2	1-0	0-1
14/5	2	2-0	1-1
19/20	2	3-0	1-1
20/1	2	2-0	1-2
21/2	2	0-0	0-1
22/3	2	2-0	0-2
23/4	2	1-0	2-1
24/5	2	0-1	2-4
56/7	2	1-5	4-1
62/3	1	0-2	1-5
70/1	2	0-1	0-4

FA Cup

Season	Rd	Home	Away
21/2	R1		0-2
62/3	R5	0-1	
63/4	R3		3-2
71/2	R4		2-0

LINCOLN CITY

Season	Div	Home	Away
05/6	2	3-0	3-2
06/7	2	1-1	0-3
07/8	2	2-0	2-2
09/10	2	1-2	0-4
10/1	2	2-0	0-0
12/3	2	1-2	1-1
13/4	2	5-1	0-0
14/5	2	3-1	0-1
19/20	2	1-0	1-2
56/7	2	2-1	2-0
57/8	2	1-0	0-2
58/9	2	0-0	0-2
59/60	2	4-0	2-2
60/1	2	1-2	0-2

LIVERPOOL

Season	Div	Home	Away
56/7	2	0-4	0-1
57/8	2	1-0	0-3
58/9	2	1-3	0-3
59/60	2	2-0	3-4
60/1	2	1-3	0-5
61/2	2	2-2	3-3
62/3	1	2-1	0-5

FA Cup

Season	Rd	Home	Away
59/60	R3		1-2

LUTON TOWN

Season	Div	Home	Away
29/30	3s	6-1	2-1
30/1	3s	3-2	1-0
31/2	3s	0-0	5-1
32/3	3s	0-0	1-4
33/4	3s	1-1	0-2
34/5	3s	1-1	0-3
35/6	3s	3-0	3-5
36/7	3s	0-2	0-2
60/1	2	2-1	1-0
61/2	2	0-0	3-1
68/9	3	0-0	1-2
69/70	3	1-0	2-3
70/1	2	1-2	0-4
71/2	2	0-0	0-2
72/3	2	0-1	1-1
73/4	2	2-0	1-3

FA Cup

Season	Rd	Home	Away
30/1	R1	2-4	2-2

MANCHESTER CITY

Season	Div	Home	Away
09/10	2	3-2	1-2
26/7	2	2-4	1-6
27/8	2	0-2	3-5
62/3	1	1-1	0-2
63/4	2	0-2	0-2
64/5	2	4-3	0-6
65/6	2	2-2	0-5

FA Cup

Season	Rd	Home	Away
19/20	R1		1-4
25/6	R6	1-6	

MANCHESTER UNITED

Season	Div	Home	Away
05/6	2	0-1	0-4
22/3	2	1-1	0-0
23/4	2	1-0	2-2
24/5	2	0-1	2-4
62/3	1	1-0	1-3

MANSFIELD TOWN			
31/2	3s	4-0	3-4
37/8	3s	1-2	1-3
38/9	3s	0-0	0-1
46/7	3s	3-1	3-1
66/7	3	4-2	1-1
67/8	3	0-0	0-0
68/9	3	1-0	2-0
69/70	3	1-0	1-4

MERTHYR TYDFIL			
29/30	3s	1-0	1-0

MIDDLESBOROUGH			
24/5	2	0-1	1-1
25/6	2	1-0	2-1
26/7	2	2-3	0-6
28/9	2	3-0	0-4
56/7	2	1-1	2-1
57/8	2	4-0	0-2
58/9	2	5-2	2-4
59/60	2	5-0	2-2
60/1	2	1-1	0-2
61/2	2	2-0	3-2
63/4	2	3-2	0-2
64/5	2	1-1	0-2
65/6	2	2-3	1-2
66/7	3	2-0	1-3
70/1	2	0-0	1-0
71/2	2	1-1	0-1
72/3	2	2-0	2-3
73/4	2	0-0	2-3

FA Cup			
25/6	R4	4-2	
35/6	R4		0-3

MILLWALL			
28/9	2	1-1	0-2
34/5	3s	2-1	1-1
35/6	3s	1-0	0-1
36/7	3s	1-0	1-2
37/8	3s	2-1	0-3
48/9	3s	0-0	2-2
49/50	3s	1-1	1-3
50/1	3s	0-2	1-3
51/2	3s	0-0	0-2
52/3	3s	1-4	0-0
53/4	3s	2-2	3-0
55/6	3s	2-1	0-5
70/1	2	0-0	1-0
71/2	2	2-2	1-2
72/3	2	3-1	0-2
73/4	2	1-1	1-0

FA Cup			
14/5	R1		1-2
22/3	R1		0-2

NELSON			
23/4	2	5-1	1-1

NEWCASTLE UNITED			
61/2	2	2-0	0-0
63/4	2	1-0	0-3
64/5	2	2-1	0-5

FA Cup			
08/9	R1		0-5
25/6	R5	2-0	
29/30	R4		1-3

League Cup			
62/3	R2	4-2	1-1

NEWPORT COUNTY			
29/30	3s	3-1	0-0
30/1	3s	3-1	1-1
32/3	3s	3-1	2-0
33/4	3s	3-0	1-1
34/5	3s	4-0	3-3
35/6	3s	4-0	3-2
36/7	3s	1-2	1-1
37/8	3s	0-2	1-3
38/9	3s	1-3	1-2
47/8	3s	2-2	2-3
48/9	3s	5-2	2-3
49/50	3s	2-1	2-3
50/1	3s	0-3	0-0
51/2	3s	1-1	0-1
52/3	3s	2-1	1-0
53/4	3s	3-0	1-1
54/5	3s	1-2	2-1
55/6	3s	3-1	0-3

NORTHAMPTON TOWN			
29/30	3s	0-0	0-3
30/1	3s	2-2	0-0
31/2	3s	3-2	3-4
32/3	3s	2-2	0-3
33/4	3s	5-1	0-3
34/5	3s	3-2	1-3
35/6	3s	4-0	0-2
36/7	3s	3-1	1-1
37/8	3s	1-0	0-2
38/9	3s	3-0	0-3
46/7	3s	2-1	1-4
47/8	3s	5-0	1-1
48/9	3s	0-3	1-4
49/50	3s	1-0	0-3
50/1	3s	1-0	3-3
51/2	3s	2-1	0-4
52/3	3s	0-1	1-3
53/4	3s	2-0	2-2
54/5	3s	2-1	2-2
55/6	3s	1-1	1-0
63/4	2	0-0	2-1
64/5	2	2-2	0-2
67/8	3	1-3	1-2
68/9	3	0-0	1-4

NORWICH CITY			
29/30	3s	0-0	0-1
30/1	3s	2-0	0-2
31/2	3s	1-3	2-3
32/3	3s	0-0	0-2
33/4	3s	3-2	0-3
46/7	3s	3-0	0-5
47/8	3s	2-1	0-3
48/9	3s	0-3	0-0
49/50	3s	1-2	0-4
50/1	3s	3-1	1-3
51/2	3s	3-3	0-1
52/3	3s	3-1	1-5
53/4	3s	3-1	1-3
54/5	3s	1-2	1-1
55/6	3s	2-2	2-2
60/1	2	1-0	2-3
61/2	2	2-0	0-0
63/4	2	1-1	2-1
64/5	2	2-3	0-2
65/6	2	0-0	1-2
70/1	2	1-0	2-4
71/2	2	1-2	0-0

FA Cup			
65/6	R3	1-3	

NOTTINGHAM FOREST			
06/7	2	0-1	0-4
11/2	2	0-2	0-3
12/3	2	2-2	0-0
13/4	2	3-1	1-1
14/5	2	0-0	1-0
19/20	2	1-0	1-2
20/1	2	2-1	1-1
21/2	2	1-2	0-2
25/6	2	0-1	0-1
26/7	2	2-2	1-1
27/8	2	2-2	3-4
28/9	2	1-4	0-0
49/50	3s	1-1	1-2
50/1	3s	0-4	1-0
56/7	2	1-4	2-1
62/3	1	0-1	1-1
72/3	2	3-0	1-2
73/4	2	2-1	1-2

FA Cup			
13/4	R1	2-2	1-0
24/5	R1		0-1
70/1	R4	0-1	1-1

NOTTS COUNTY			
13/4	2	1-0	0-3
20/1	2	3-0	1-3
21/2	2	2-1	0-0
22/3	2	2-1	1-3
26/7	2	2-1	1-3

27/8	2	0-1	0-3
28/9	2	2-2	0-2
30/1	3s	1-4	0-5
35/6	3s	0-2	0-2
36/7	3s	1-1	0-0
37/8	3s	2-0	0-1
38/9	3s	1-1	0-1
46/7	3s	1-3	2-1
47/8	3s	2-1	4-1
48/9	3s	3-1	1-2
49/50	3s	1-4	1-7
56/7	2	2-2	3-1
57/8	2	2-2	1-0
73/4	2	1-1	4-2

FA Cup

46/7	R1	1-2	

League Cup

71/2	R1	1-1	1-3

OLDHAM ATHLETIC

07/8	2	2-0	1-4
08/9	2	2-0	0-2
09/10	2	1-2	0-5
23/4	2	1-2	0-1
24/5	2	5-1	1-2
25/6	2	1-2	1-1
26/7	2	3-1	2-5
27/8	2	2-0	0-5
28/9	2	2-0	1-1
66/7	3	2-2	1-3
67/8	3	0-2	2-2
68/9	3	3-0	1-3

OXFORD UNITED

66/7	3	2-1	0-0
67/8	3	1-0	0-2
70/1	2	0-0	1-0
71/2	2	1-1	1-1
72/3	2	1-1	1-2
73/4	2	1-1	1-1

PETERBOROUGH UNITED

66/7	3	1-1	2-0
67/8	3	3-0	2-3

PLYMOUTH ARGYLE

29/30	3s	0-2	0-3
50/1	3s	1-2	1-2
51/2	3s	1-0	0-3
59/60	2	2-3	0-1
60/1	2	1-1	2-3
61/2	2	1-2	1-2
63/4	2	1-0	2-2
64/5	2	2-0	1-1
65/6	2	0-1	1-1
68/9	3	1-2	1-2
69/70	3	4-1	0-1

FA Cup

55/6	R3	1-0	

PORTSMOUTH

24/5	2	1-1	2-0
25/6	2	1-1	2-3
26/7	2	4-5	1-1
59/60	2	1-2	1-1
60/1	2	2-1	2-1
63/4	2	3-6	3-4
64/5	2	5-2	1-1
65/6	2	0-0	1-4
70/1	2	1-1	1-1
71/2	2	2-1	2-3
72/3	2	0-1	0-1
73/4	2	2-1	0-0

FA Cup

73/4	R4	1-1	0-0
		0-2	

(2nd replay at
Crystal Palace)

PORT VALE

05/6	2	1-3	1-2
06/7	2	1-1	2-3
19/20	2	2-1	2-4
20/1	2	0-0	0-4
21/2	2	2-0	0-3
22/3	2	0-0	1-3
23/4	2	1-1	0-1
24/5	2	3-1	2-4
25/6	2	1-2	2-4
26/7	2	1-2	0-3
27/8	2	0-1	0-0
28/9	2	1-0	0-3
38/9	3s	1-0	1-1
46/7	3s	5-3	1-2
47/8	3s	0-0	0-3
48/9	3s	2-0	0-3
49/50	3s	1-0	0-2
50/1	3s	2-3	1-3
51/2	3s	2-0	0-3
56/7	2	3-2	2-1

FA Cup

26/7	R3	1-1	1-5
53/4	R6	0-1	

PRESTON NORTH END

12/3	2	1-2	1-0
14/5	2	1-1	2-2
25/6	2	1-1	1-4
26/7	2	1-1	2-2
27/8	2	1-1	0-0
28/9	2	1-0	2-5

61/2	2	0-2	2-3
63/4	2	2-2	0-0
64/5	2	2-1	0-3
65/6	2	2-2	2-1
71/2	2	3-2	1-1
72/3	2	1-2	0-0
73/4	2	2-2	1-0

QPR

29/30	3s	2-4	1-1
30/1	3s	2-3	2-4
31/2	3s	3-0	2-3
32/3	3s	2-2	1-2
33/4	3s	2-2	0-2
34/5	3s	3-1	3-6
35/6	3s	1-0	0-4
36/7	3s	0-0	1-2
37/8	3s	1-1	2-3
38/9	3s	2-1	1-1
46/7	3s	1-1	0-2
47/8	3s	1-3	2-1
52/3	3s	5-0	1-0
53/4	3s	2-2	1-2
54/5	3s	3-0	0-2
55/6	3s	7-1	1-0
66/7	3	0-0	1-4
70/1	2	0-1	1-5
71/2	2	2-0	0-1
72/3	2	2-2	1-3

READING

26/7	2	5-1	1-0
27/8	2	3-0	0-4
28/9	2	1-1	2-4
31/2	3s	2-2	0-5
32/3	3s	2-5	1-3
33/4	3s	2-3	0-4
34/5	3s	2-1	0-0
35/6	3s	1-0	1-4
36/7	3s	3-2	1-1
37/8	3s	1-1	0-2
38/9	3s	1-2	2-2
46/7	3s	3-3	0-2
47/8	3s	2-2	2-6
48/9	3s	0-1	0-3
49/50	3s	2-1	1-5
50/1	3s	2-0	0-4
51/2	3s	0-4	1-1
52/3	3s	1-1	0-2
53/4	3s	2-1	1-1
54/5	3s	2-0	2-0
55/6	3s	1-0	1-0
66/7	3	3-2	0-1
67/8	3	1-0	2-4
68/9	3	4-2	1-0
69/70	3	0-1	2-3

FA Cup

57/8	R3	1-0	

ROCHDALE

69/70	3	2-2	3-0

ROTHERHAM UNITED

19/20	2	1-2	1-3
20/1	2	2-0	0-0
21/2	2	1-2	0-2
22/3	2	5-1	0-0
56/7	2	2-1	0-2
57/8	2	6-2	2-2
58/9	2	2-0	1-1
59/60	2	2-3	1-1
60/1	2	2-1	1-2
61/2	2	1-1	1-2
63/4	2	0-2	4-2
64/5	2	2-1	0-3
65/6	2	1-4	1-2
68/9	3	3-3	1-3
69/70	3	1-1	0-0

SCUNTHORPE UNITED

58/9	2	2-1	0-2
59/60	2	1-1	1-2
60/1	2	2-1	2-2
61/2	2	0-1	2-0
63/4	2	2-2	0-0
66/7	3	3-1	2-2
67/8	3	2-1	1-1

SHEFFIELD UNITED

56/7	2	1-2	3-2
57/8	2	0-1	2-0
58/9	2	1-1	3-2
59/60	2	1-1	2-0
60/1	2	1-4	1-4
62/3	1	2-2	0-2
70/1	2	3-1	1-3

SHEFFIELD WEDNESDAY

20/1	2	1-0	1-1
21/2	2	1-1	0-0
22/3	2	2-2	1-4
23/4	2	0-0	0-1
24/5	2	1-0	0-0
25/6	2	0-0	0-3
58/9	2	0-2	0-2
62/3	1	2-4	1-3
70/1	2	1-1	1-2
71/2	2	0-3	1-3
72/3	2	3-2	0-2
73/4	2	0-1	2-1

FA Cup

60/1	R5	0-2	

SHREWSBURY TOWN

51/2	3s	4-1	0-3
52/3	3s	0-0	0-2
53/4	3s	2-0	3-3
54/5	3s	5-0	2-0
55/6	3s	5-2	4-1
66/7	3	2-2	1-6
67/8	3	1-1	2-2
68/9	3	4-0	0-1
69/70	3	1-0	1-1

SOUTHAMPTON

22/3	2	1-0	0-2
23/4	2	0-0	0-5
24/5	2	1-0	0-2
25/6	2	2-1	0-2
26/7	2	1-0	2-1
27/8	2	2-0	3-1
28/9	2	1-1	0-2
53/4	3s	1-4	1-4
54/5	3s	4-1	0-1
55/6	3s	4-0	2-1
60/1	2	1-1	1-1
61/2	2	1-3	2-1
63/4	2	1-0	0-3
64/5	2	0-0	2-2
65/6	2	1-1	0-1

FA Cup

28/9	R3	2-1	0-0
60/1	R4	1-0	
64/5	R3	1-3	

SOUTHEND UNITED

29/30	3s	1-1	1-4
30/1	3s	3-1	0-2
31/2	3s	2-4	3-1
32/3	3s	0-0	3-3
33/4	3s	5-2	1-2
34/5	3s	3-0	2-0
35/6	3s	3-0	1-2
36/7	3s	3-0	0-0
37/8	3s	1-1	2-1
38/9	3s	5-0	0-1
46/7	3s	1-1	0-0
47/8	3s	2-0	1-2
48/9	3s	2-0	2-2
49/50	3s	2-2	0-2
50/1	3s	1-1	1-0
51/2	3s	1-4	0-1
52/3	3s	3-0	0-1
53/4	3s	1-1	1-2
54/5	3s	5-1	2-1
55/6	3s	3-0	0-0

FA Cup

07/8	R3	1-1	1-3
49/50	R1	0-2	

SOUTHPORT

67/8	3	3-0	0-0
68/9	3	0-2	2-2
69/70	3	3-2	0-1

STOCKPORT COUNTY

05/6	2	1-0	3-3
06/7	2	1-1	1-1
07/8	2	4-1	1-6
08/9	2	5-0	1-1
09/10	2	2-0	0-3
10/1	2	1-0	3-0
11/2	2	4-2	1-1
12/3	2	4-1	0-2
13/4	2	1-1	1-0
14/5	2	3-0	0-2
19/20	2	2-1	1-3
20/1	2	5-0	0-6
22/3	2	0-2	2-0
23/4	2	1-1	0-2
24/5	2	1-1	1-0
25/6	2	2-1	2-3
67/8	3	2-2	0-2
68/9	3	2-0	2-5
69/70	3	3-0	2-0

League Cup

61/2	R1		1-0

STOKE CITY

07/8	2	3-0	0-3
19/20	2	2-1	0-2
20/1	2	3-2	1-0
21/2	2	1-0	0-0
23/4	2	0-2	1-0
24/5	2	0-2	1-0
25/6	2	4-0	0-0
27/8	2	3-2	0-2
28/9	2	1-0	1-3
56/7	2	2-2	1-7
57/8	2	0-2	3-1
58/9	2	0-1	2-3
59/60	2	2-1	1-2
60/1	2	3-1	2-1
61/2	2	3-0	1-0

SUNDERLAND

58/9	2	6-0	0-4
59/60	2	1-1	4-1
60/1	2	0-1	1-4
61/2	2	1-1	1-2
63/4	2	2-5	1-4
70/1	2	1-0	0-1
71/2	2	5-0	0-2
72/3	2	1-1	0-1
73/4	2	2-1	1-1

FA Cup

12/3	R1		0-6
70/1	R3		3-0

SWANSEA CITY

25/6	2	2-0	0-0
26/7	2	1-0	2-3
27/8	2	1-1	0-5
28/9	2	1-2	1-0
47/8	3s	1-0	0-5
48/9	3s	3-1	1-3
56/7	2	3-0	0-1
57/8	2	5-1	2-1
58/9	2	0-0	3-3
59/60	2	2-1	0-1
60/1	2	2-2	0-1
61/2	2	1-0	3-1
63/4	2	4-0	0-1
64/5	2	2-3	5-2
66/7	3	1-0	0-2

FA Cup

23/4	R1	1-1	1-1
		1-2	
		(2nd replay at	
		Tottenham)	

SWINDON TOWN

29/30	3s	2-1	0-0
30/1	3s	2-3	1-5
31/2	3s	4-2	3-2
32/3	3s	7-1	3-3
33/4	3s	1-0	0-3
34/5	3s	2-0	1-1
35/6	3s	1-2	2-2
36/7	3s	1-1	3-1
37/8	3s	1-0	0-1
38/9	3s	5-0	0-2
46/7	3s	0-0	0-2
47/8	3s	0-3	1-0
48/9	3s	1-1	1-1
49/50	3s	1-3	1-0
50/1	3s	2-1	0-2
51/2	3s	1-0	0-2
52/3	3s	2-2	1-1
53/4	3s	1-1	1-2
54/5	3s	1-0	0-0
55/6	3s	4-0	2-1
63/4	2	2-1	0-5
64/5	2	0-3	0-1
66/7	3	0-0	1-5
67/8	3	0-0	0-5
68/9	3	1-0	0-1
70/1	2	1-0	1-1
71/2	2	0-1	2-2
72/3	2	1-0	1-3
73/4	2	0-0	2-2

FA Cup

27/8	R3		1-2

THAMES

30/1	3s	2-1	0-3
31/2	3s	1-1	3-3

TORQUAY UNITED

29/30	3s	1-1	5-0
30/1	3s	4-0	2-5
31/2	3s	1-3	0-3
32/3	3s	1-4	1-1
33/4	3s	4-1	1-2
34/5	3s	3-1	2-4
35/6	3s	1-1	0-1
36/7	3s	2-0	1-4
37/8	3s	2-0	1-3
38/9	3s	3-0	1-2
46/7	3s	0-1	2-3
47/8	3s	4-1	1-0
48/9	3s	3-1	1-7

49/50	3s	2-1	1-4
50/1	3s	5-1	1-2
51/2	3s	0-1	1-1
52/3	3s	4-1	0-5
53/4	3s	3-2	3-2
54/5	3s	2-1	7-2
55/6	3s	3-2	3-1
66/7	3	0-0	1-1
67/8	3	0-2	1-1
68/9	3	0-1	0-0
69/70	3	1-1	1-0

FA Cup

36/7	R1	2-1	
37/8	R1		2-1

TOTTENHAM HOTSPURS

08/9	2	0-0	1-0
19/20	2	0-4	1-2
28/9	2	2-3	1-2
62/3	1	1-5	0-2

TRANMERE ROVERS

67/8	3	0-1	0-3
68/9	3	0-0	0-3
69/70	3	2-0	1-1

FA Cup

53/4	R3	4-1	2-2

WALSALL

29/30	3s	1-1	1-0
30/1	3s	2-5	2-4
36/7	3s	2-2	2-3
37/8	3s	2-2	0-2
38/9	3s	1-1	1-5
46/7	3s	1-0	1-3
47/8	3s	1-3	0-1
48/9	3s	1-1	3-2
49/50	3s	2-2	2-1
50/1	3s	2-1	1-1
51/2	3s	3-0	4-2
52/3	3s	4-1	0-1
53/4	3s	2-1	2-4
54/5	3s	1-0	4-1
55/6	3s	4-0	2-0
61/2	2	3-0	5-1
66/7	3	0-2	1-1
67/8	3	2-0	0-5
68/9	3	0-0	1-2
69/70	3	2-0	0-2

FA Cup

33/4	R2	2-0	0-0
38/9	R2		2-4
69/70	R1	0-2	0-0

WATFORD

29/30	3s	1-1	0-3
30/1	3s	4-0	2-1
31/2	3s	2-2	1-2
32/3	3s	2-0	1-1
33/4	3s	2-3	0-6
34/5	3s	1-1	0-5
35/6	3s	0-2	1-1
36/7	3s	1-1	1-2
37/8	3s	1-1	0-2
38/9	3s	0-0	0-1
46/7	3s	3-1	1-3
47/8	3s	0-2	1-2
48/9	3s	1-0	1-2
49/50	3s	0-0	1-2
50/1	3s	1-2	0-2
51/2	3s	0-0	1-0
52/3	3s	2-0	1-0
53/4	3s	1-1	1-3
54/5	3s	0-1	3-1
55/6	3s	3-1	4-0
66/7	3	1-1	3-1
67/8	3	0-1	1-1
68/9	3	1-1	0-0
70/1	2	1-1	0-0
71/2	2	1-0	1-0

League Cup

72/3	R1	2-0	

WEST BROMWICH ALBION

05/6	2	0-2	1-1
06/7	2	1-1	0-5
07/8	2	2-2	0-3
08/9	2	1-0	0-1
09/10	2	1-3	0-3
10/1	2	0-0	0-3
27/8	2	0-0	1-4
28/9	2	0-2	1-3
62/3	1	2-3	1-2
73/4	2	2-0	0-1

FA Cup

09/10	R1		0-2

WEST HAM UNITED

19/20	2	1-0	1-0
20/1	2	0-1	0-1
21/2	2	0-0	2-1
22/3	2	0-2	0-1
56/7	2	1-2	1-2
57/8	2	1-4	2-3
62/3	1	2-0	0-2

FA Cup

63/4	R4	1-1	0-3

League Cup
63/4   R2   1-2

WOLVERHAMPTON WANDERERS

Season	Div		
06/7	2	4-0	1-6
07/8	2	1-1	0-2
08/9	2	1-3	1-5
09/10	2	1-0	1-3
10/1	2	3-1	0-1
11/2	2	1-0	1-0
12/3	2	0-0	1-1
13/4	2	2-2	1-2
14/5	2	1-1	0-0
19/20	2	0-0	2-1
20/1	2	0-1	2-0
21/2	2	1-0	2-0
22/3	2	4-1	3-1
24/5	2	2-1	2-1
25/6	2	2-1	0-3
26/7	2	2-0	0-5
27/8	2	0-0	3-5
28/9	2	2-0	2-3
62/3	1	0-4	1-2
65/6	2	0-3	1-2

League Cup
72/3   R2   1-2

WORKINGTON
66/7   3   2-1   1-3

FA Cup
54/5   R2   0-1

WREXHAM
FA Cup
51/2   R2   3-2   1-1
71/2   R3   3-0

YORK CITY
FA Cup
37/8   R2   2-2   0-1

League Cup
73/4   R3   1-1   1-2

ORIENT'S RECORD AGAINST NON-LEAGUE CLUBS IN FA CUP
(Orient's score shown first)

29/30   R1   Folkestone Town (H) 0-0 (A) 2-2 (At Highbury) 4-1
         R2   Northfleet (H) 2-0
33/4   R1   Epsom Town (H) 4-2

34/5   R1   Ashford Town (A) 4-1
35/6   R2   Folkestone Town (A) 2-1
38/9   R1   Hayes (H) 3-1
45/6   R1   Newport I.O.W. Leg 1 (H) 2-1 Leg 2 (A) 0-2
48/9   R1   Dartford (A) 3-2
51/2   R1   Gorleston (H) 2-2 (A) 0-0 (At Highbury) 5-4
53/4   R1   Kettering (H) 3-0
         R2   Weymouth (H) 4-0
54/5   R1   Frome Town (A) 3-0
55/6   R1   Lovells Athletic (H) 7-1
66/7   R1   Lowestoft Town (H) 2-1
67/8   R1   Weymouth (A) 2-0
         R2   Boston United (A) 1-1 (H) 2-1

The following are also Orient's FA Cup results against non-League opponents (these have already been shown in O's record against League Clubs). These results were against clubs who were then non-League, but now League clubs.

07/8   R3   Southend United (H) 1-1 (A) 1-3
13/4   R2   Brighton & H.A. (A) 1-3
14/5   R1   Millwall (A) 1-2
47/8   R1   Gillingham (A) 0-1

RECORD IN THE FOOTBALL LEAGUE

Season	Div.	P.	W.	D.	L.	F.	A.	Pts.	Pos.
05/6	2	38	7	7	24	35	78	21	20
06/7	2	38	11	8	19	45	67	30	17
07/8	2	38	11	10	17	40	65	32	14
08/9	2	38	12	9	17	37	49	33	15
09/10	2	38	12	6	20	37	60	30	16
10/1	2	38	19	7	12	44	35	45	4
11/2	2	38	21	3	14	61	44	45	4
12/3	2	38	10	14	14	34	47	34	14
13/4	2	38	16	11	11	47	35	43	6
14/5	2	38	16	9	13	50	48	41	9
15-9	No Competition								
19/20	2	42	16	6	20	51	59	38	15
20/1	2	42	16	13	13	43	42	45	7
21/2	2	42	15	9	18	43	50	39	15
22/3	2	42	12	12	18	40	50	36	19
23/4	2	42	14	15	13	40	36	43	10
24/5	2	42	14	12	16	42	42	40	11
25/6	2	42	12	9	21	50	65	33	20
26/7	2	42	12	7	23	60	96	31	20
27/8	2	42	11	12	19	55	85	34	20
28/9	2	42	12	8	22	45	72	32	22
29/30	3s	42	14	13	15	55	62	41	12
30/1	3s	42	14	7	21	63	91	35	19
31/2	3s	42	12	11	19	77	90	35	16
32/3	3s	42	8	13	21	59	93	29	20
33/4	3s	42	16	10	16	75	69	42	11
34/5	3s	42	15	10	17	65	65	40	14
35/6	3s	42	16	6	20	55	61	38	14
36/7	3s	42	14	15	13	52	52	43	12
37/8	3s	42	13	7	22	42	61	33	19
38/9	3s	42	11	13	18	53	55	35	20
39/46	No Competition								
46/7	3s	42	12	8	22	54	75	32	19
47/8	3s	42	13	10	19	51	73	36	17
48/9	3s	42	11	12	19	58	80	34	19
49/50	3s	42	12	11	19	53	85	35	18
50/1	3s	46	15	8	23	53	75	38	19
51/2	3s	46	16	9	21	55	68	41	18
52/3	3s	46	16	10	20	68	73	42	14
53/4	3s	46	18	11	17	79	73	47	11
54/5	3s	46	26	9	11	89	47	61	2
55/6	3s	46	29	8	9	106	49	66	1
56/7	2	42	15	10	17	66	84	40	15
57/8	2	42	18	5	19	77	79	41	12
58/9	2	42	14	8	20	71	78	36	17
59/60	2	42	15	14	13	76	61	44	10
60/1	2	42	14	8	20	55	78	36	19
61/2	2	42	22	10	10	69	40	54	2
62/3	1	42	6	9	27	37	81	21	22
63/4	2	42	13	10	19	54	72	36	16
64/5	2	42	12	11	19	50	72	35	19
65/6	2	42	5	13	24	38	80	23	22
66/7	3	46	13	18	15	58	68	44	14
67/8	3	46	12	17	17	46	62	41	19
68/9	3	46	14	14	18	51	58	42	18
69/70	3	46	25	12	9	67	36	62	1
70/1	2	42	9	16	17	29	51	34	17
71/2	2	42	14	9	19	50	61	37	17
72/3	2	42	12	12	18	49	53	36	15
73/4	2	42	15	18	9	55	42	48	4

Orient's League record up to the start of the 74/5 season reads as follows:

Played	Won	Drawn	Lost
2391	812	588	991

For	Against		Points
3119	3606		2212

League Appearances (05-74)

(Substitutes in brackets) (G goalkeeper, D defender, M midfield, F forward.)

Name	Pos	Years	Apps
Ackerman, A.	D	66-68	4
Adams, G.	F	48-50	4
Affleck, D.	D	35-37	66
Aldous, S.	D	50-58	302
Allen, A.	M	33-34	1
Allen, J.	F	37-38	5
Allison, W.	M	31-32	14
Ames, L.	F	26-31	14
Anderson, T.	DF	67-68	8(1)
Andrews, J.	F	56-59	35
Arber, R.	D	68-74	31
Archell, G.	F	67-70	5(2)
Archibald, J.	M	23-26	49
Armitage, K.	D	46-47	7
Armstrong, J.	D	26-28	2
Ashton, H.	D	26-27	5
Bacon, C.	M	46-50	118
Bailey, D.	F	22-23	18
Baily, E.	F	58-61	29
Ballard, E.	D	46-47 & 52-53	26
Banner, A.	D	48-53	165
Barr, J.	M	22-23	8
Bartlett, F.	D	37-38	96
Batten, H.	F	27-29	31
Baynham, J.	F	46-48	60
Beale, P.	F	08-09	5
Bell, J.	D	24-26	2
Bell, M.	M	07-10	88
Benson, C.	F	12-13	1
Best, J.	F	31-33	51
Bevan, F.	F	09-14	128
Biggs, A.	F	58-60	4
Bishop, S.	D	52-65	296
Black, R.	M	38-46	23
Blackwell, H.	G	30-32	16
Blair, J.	F	49-53	107
Blatchford, P.	F	51-54	59
Bliss, H.	F	22-25	70
Blizzard, L.	M	50-57	221
Bloomfield, J.	F	68-69	43(2)
Boden, J.	M	05-06	27
Bolland, G.	F	62-64	63
Bolton, J.	M	30-32	38
Bourne, R.	F	05-07	56
Bower, W.	G	05-18	171
Bowtell, S.	G	66-73	8
Bowyer, I.	F	71-73	75
Bowyer, W.	F	19-20	21
Boyd, H.	M	36-37	2
Boyle, P.	D	05-06	10
Bradbrook, P.	F	68-71	70(2)
Bradbury, G.	D	20-22	31
Bradbury, T.	M	66-67	25(2)
Bradley, J.	F	20-21	5
Brahan, L.	D	55-56	1
Bratby, J.	F	20-23	26
Brinton, J.	F	48-49	4
Broadbent, W.	M	25-32	200
Brooks, C.	D	36-38	4
Brown, A.	F	05-06	4
Brown, C.	M	36-37	1
Brown, E.	F	59-61	63
Brown, T.	M	50-53	98
Brown, W.	D	44-48	26
Brown, W.C.	F	46-47	2
Bruce, J.	G	32-33	19
Bruce, R.	F	51-52	1
Bryant, E.	F	51-52	12
Buchanan, D.	M	06-08	65
Burgess, M.	F	53-56	32
Burridge, P.	F	58-61	6
Butler, J.	G	05-06	20
Cairney, C.	M	50-51	4
Calderhead, W.	M	20-21	1
Caldwell, J.	M	07-08	12
Caldwell, T.	F	07-08	7
Campbell, A.	M	26-28	23
Campbell, H.	F	35-36	9
Campbell, J.	F	29-30	25
Campbell, J.	F	49-50	5
Candy, G.	F	08-10	3
Canvin, C.	M	46-47	3
Carey, P.	M	56-60	34
Carey, W.	M	26-27	3
Carrington, J.	G	19-20	1
Carter, W.	F	64-67	26
Cater, R.	M	51-52	14
Chapman, J.	F	19-20	9
Chapman, V.	F	47-49	31
Charlton, S.	D	52-55 & 58-65	367
Chisem, F.	M	32-33	1
Clark, D.	D	61-65	4
Clark, H.	F	24-26	4
Clark, J.	D	46-47	18
Clegg, J.	G	13-14	8
Cochran, A.	G	60-63	1
Cock, D.	F	25-27	64
Cockle, H.	F	20-21	20
Codling, A.	F	36-38	32
Codling, R.	M	05-06	28
Collins, E.	F	27-29	40
Connelly, E.	F	48-50	32
Cook, R.	M	55-58	2
Cooper, K.	F	32-33	4
Corkindale, J.	F	26-29	96
Coull, G.	D	34-35	4
Crawford, E.	F	33-43	199
Crompton, W.	D	33-35	79
Cropper, A.	F	30-32	27
Cross, R.	F	68	4(2)
Crossan, E.	F	60-61	8
Dale, G.	G	19-21	1
Dalrymple, R.	F	10-20	139
Davidson, D.	D	46-50	83
Davies, David.	F	53-55	4
Davies, Dudley.	F	50-52	17
Davies, R.	G	63-64 & 65-66	27
Davin, M.	F	33-34	15
Davis, E.	G	12-13	4
Davis, F.	F	35-36	2
Dawson, T.	D	32-33	19
Deeley, N.	F	62-64	73
Dennison, R.	F	26-29	69
Denton, F.	F	20-22	3
Deverall, H.	M	48-53	114
Dimmock, J.	F	32-33	18
Dix, J.	F	10-15	147
Dixon, T.	M	19-27	232
Dodds, L.	F	37-39	53
Dodgin, W.	M	37-39	61
Dominy, A.	F	29-30	5
Dougal, D.	M	05-07	51
Dryden, J.	F	48-50	40
Dryden, W.	F	12-13	13
Dudley, S.	F	29-30	11
Duffus, J.	M	22-23	10
Duffus, R.	D	22-24	1
Duffy, B.	M	26-29	68
Dunmore, D.	F	61-65	147
Dunn, H.	F	24-26	4
Dunne, T.	F	64-65	1
Dyson, B.	F	68-73	154(6)
Eadie, D.	F	67	2
Eagles, A.	D	57-61	75
Earl, S.	D	53-57	33
Earle, S.	F	32-33	15
Eastman, G.	D	28-30	13
Edmonds, A.	DF	29-32	88
Edwards, E.	F	29-32 & 35-36	6
Edwards, S.	F	53-56	2
Ellis, F.	D	32-33	27
Elwood, J.	F	58-66	102(2)
Emery, H.	G	31-33	62
Evans, J.	D	50-56	149
Evans, N.	D	12-15	111
Evans, T.	D	24-28 & 30-32	81
Evenson, I.	M	05-07	64
Facey, K.	MF	52-62	301
Farley, A.	D	45-48	15
Farrell, F.	F	37-40	2
Farrell, V.	F	34-37	79
Fellowes, W.	D	33-35	78
Fenton, J.	D	46-47	7
Ferry, G.	D	65-66	42
Findlay, A.	M	26-27	2
Finlayson, J.	D	33-35	12

Name	Pos	Years	Apps
Mallett, J.	M	53-58	27
Mancini, T.	D	67-71	167
Manns, T.	D	34-35	3
Mansley, C.	M	52-53	10
Martin, W.	F	06-08	61
Mason, R.	F	63-64	23
Massey, R.	F	67-70	58(5)
Mayson, J.	F	33-36	29
McAleer, J.	F	35-36	18
McClellan, S.	F	58-59	12
McCombe, J.	F	36-38	44
McCrae, J.	M	30-31	3
McDonald, R.	D	27-29	37
McDonald, T.	F	59-65	151
McEwan, W.	F	50-51	21
McFadden, R.	F	11-15	137
McGeachy, J.	F	48-51	75
McGeorge, K.	M	05-06	14
McGeorge, J.	F	64-66	16
McKay, J.	F	24-26	8
McKechnie, J.	D	23-26	46
McKeenan, A.	F	46-47	1
McKnight, P.	M	54-61	162
McLaughan, R.	F	25-26	19
McLean, R.	F	08-10	39
McMahon, E.	F	13-14	3
McMahon, P.	M	51-59	64
McMillan, S.	F	28-30	23
Menlove, B.	F	29-30	1
Merritt, G.	F	45-47	1
Metchick, D.	F	64-67	75
Meynell, W.	D	09-11	16
Miles, I.	F	34-37	73
Millington, J.	F	34-35	2
Mills, T.	F	29-34	120
Morgan, S.	F	53-56	96
Morley, E.	D	28-32	71
Morrad, F.	F	46-47	25
Morris, D.	F	33-34	13
Morris, J.	G	14-15	4
Morrison, M.	G	47-48	10
Moss, R.	F	68-72	2(3)
Musgrove, M.	F	62-66	83
Naylor, W.	F	47-50	65
Neary, F.	F	47-49	78
Nelson, A.	D	64-65	43
Newman, R.	F	61-62	14
Newton, R.	G	48-49	23
Nicholas, A.	F	65-66	8(1)
Nichols, J.	D	19-26	117
Nicholson, D.	F	53-58	5
Nicholson, H.	G	59-60	4
Nicholson, J.	M	19-24	145
Nunn, A.	F	20-24	19
O'Brien, G.	F	66-67	17
O'Gara, J.	F	08-09	1
Oliver, F.	F	06-13	39
Osmond, J.	D	19-23	50
Owen, T.	D	57-61	15
Pacey, D.	F	51-54	119
Pape, A.	F	24-25	24
Parker, F.	F	07-22	336
Parkinson, A.	G	67	1
Parmenter, T.	F	69-71	34(3)
Pateman, G.	F	35-36	9
Paterson, J.	F	38-39	5
Pattison, F.	F	13-14	7
Pattison, J.	F	50-51	42
Peacock, J.	M	31-33	54
Pemberton, F.	M	06-08	4
Percy, A.	F	38-39	4
Phillips, E.	F	64-65	36
Phillips, G.R.	F	32-33	3
Phillips, W.J.	F	32-33	24
Pickering, W.	M	32-33	12
Pinner, M.	G	62-65	77
Plume, R.	M	69-71	12(6)
Pole, H.	F	51-53	12
Poulton, G.	F	52-56	61
Price, T.	F	62-67	86(1)
Prior, P.	F	08-14	19
Pritchard, A.	M	38-39	1
Proudfoot, P.	M	05-06	26
Pullen, W.	F	45-51	116
Ramage, G.	G	64-65	4
Reading, J.	G	05-06	7
Reason, H.	D	05-11	93
Reed, C.	D	09-10	2
Reed, G.	D	35-36	1
Rees, W.	F	50-55	184
Reid, T.	F	26-27	8
Rennie, J.	D	38-39	6
Rennox, C.	F	21-25	101
Reynolds, W.	F	31-32	2
Richardson, J.	F	47-48	15
Richmond, W.	M	38-39	1
Riddell, N.	D	11-12	11
Riddick, G.	M	70-72	13(8)
Ridley, R.	F	14-15	17
Rigby, A.	F	33-34	70
Ritson, L.	D	46-49	84
Roach, J.	F	07-08	1
Robb, W.	M	50-51	5
Roberts, F.	F	46-47	18
Roberts, J.	M	31-32	2
Robertson, A.	G	33-35	48
Robertson, W.	G	60-63	47
Robinson, S.	D	33-34	2
Rofe, D.	D	65-72	170(1)
Rogers, W.	M	33-34	3
Rooney, R.	D	48-51	66
Rose, S.	M	22-23	3
Roseboom, E.	F	23-24	3
Rosier, H.	D	22-27	136
Rossiter, A.	F	36-38	7
Rossiter, D.	F	56-57	1
Roulson, J.	M	24-25	16
Rouse, V.	G	65-66	40
Rumbold, G.	D	37-46	52
Rutherford, J.	F	26-27	9
Sage, W.	M	27-28	12
Sales, R.	D	47-49	56
Sanders, A.	F	29-33	53
Scott, G.	F	08-15	205
Scott, J.	F	62-66	22(1)
Sealey, A.	F	59-61	4
Searle, F.	D	34-38	122
Seigel, A.	M	46-47	9
Sewell, J.	D	71-72	5(2)
Sexton, D.	F	56-58	24
Shankly, R.	F	37-44	13
Shaw, C.	F	65-66	7
Shaw, J.	F	08-09	19
Shea, D.	F	24-26	33
Shearer, J.	M	20-21	4
Shelley, G.	D	07-09 & 10-11	9
Sherratt, J.	D	49-52	37
Silvester, B.	F	11-12	1
Simmonds, C.	F	50-51	15
Simons, H.	F	05-07	7
Simpson, O.	D	67-68	36
Skelton, G.	F	47-48	3
Skivington, M.	D	49-50	5
Slater, J.	G	26-30	19
Slater, M.	F	67-70	111
Smith, A.	F	49-50	6
Smith, G.	G	14-15	2
Smith, G.	D	32-33	2
Smith, H.	F	19-25	167
Smith, H.	F	34-46	148
Smith, Jack.	F	36-37	5

Name	Pos	Years	Apps	Name	Pos	Years	Apps	Name	Pos	Years	Apps
Smith, Jim.	F	46-47	22	Taylor, W.	F	59-64	23	Vanner, R.	F	29-31	35
Smith, Jimmy.	F	55-58	37	Thacker, F.	M	06-08	34	Waite, A.	F	22-26	62
Smith, John.	M	65-66	38(1)	Thomas, E.	F	67-68	11	Waites, G.	F	58-61 & 62-63	45
Smith, K.	F	67	3	Thomas, L.	F	06-07	5				
Smith, M.	D	36-39	5	Thompson, A.	F	32-33	18	Wall, P.	D	72-73	10
Smith, W.S.	M	27-28	6	Thompson, B.	F	08-09	6	Waller, H.	M	47-48	17
Snedden, J.	D	66-68	26(1)	Thompson, T.	G	06-07	1	Walters, T.	F	38-39	23
Sorrell, D.	M	57-62 & 64-66	111	Thomson, J.	M	24-25	1	Walton, R.	D	48-51	64
				Thomson, N.	F	26-27	10	Warboys, A.	D	18-23	43
Spence, J.	D	26-30	29	Thorne, A.	F	65-66	2	Ward, F.	F	08-09	33
Spencer, A.	F	13-14	1	Tidman, O.	F	37-38	1	Ward, G.	M	63-65	44
Spottiswood, R.	M	19-20	1	Tilley, A.	F	12-13	1	Ware, E.	M	33-36	106
Steel, D.	D	14-15	23	Tolliday, S.	G	46-49	64	Waterall, A.	F	26-27	2
Stevens, G.	F	14-15	1	Tonner, J.	F	19-27	140	Watson, D.	M	31-32	2
Stewart, T.	D	06-08	50	Tonner, J.E.	D	19-20	14	Watts, E.	G	06-07	2
Still, J.	D	67-68	1	Tonner, S.	D	19-25	188	Webb, D.	D	63-66	62
Stonehouse, G.	D	11-13	3	Townley, J.	F	29-31	19	Wells, J.	F	36-37	4
Street, A.	M	66-67	1	Townrow, J.	D	19-27	254	Welton, P.	G	49-58	263
Streets, G.	D	25-28	12	Trailor, C.	M	49-51	39	Went, P.	D	65-67	48(2)
Stroud, W.	M	47-50	65	Tricker, R.	F	28-33	130	Werge, E.	F	66-68	30(3)
Surtees, A.	M	27-28	1	Tulley, F.	F	37-45	57	Whipp, P.	F	21-22 & 27-29	89
Sutherland, G.	F	49-51	43	Tulley, J.	F	09-11	5				
Taylor, A.	M	48-51	46	Turnbull, R.	F	28-30	39	White, P.	F	53-64	221
Taylor, H.	M	33-46	175	Underwood, A.	F	09-10	38	Whitehouse, B.	F	66-68	52
Taylor, J.	D	35-37	30	Van Den Eynden,I.	D	13-14	12	Whiteley, A.	F	52-54	23
Taylor, T.	D	67-70	112(2)	Vango, A.	D	32-33	23	Whittaker, J.	F	07-08	17

Orient's greatest fans? Dave Randlesome, Paul Hiscock and Alan Cockerill never miss a match

Whittaker, W.	G	07-10	90
Whyte, C.	D	38-39	6
Willemse, S.	D	56-58	59
Williams, E.	D	07-08	5
Williams, E.	F	28-29	3
Williams, J.	F	09-10	12
Williams, Jesse.	F	27-29	31
Williams, O.	F	19-24	162
Williams, R.	F	38-44	35
Williams, T.	F	21-23	26
Willingham, A.	F	10-11	1
Willis, H.	M	08-14	136
Willis, R.	G	65-67	45
Willshaw, G.	F	39-47	12
Wingham, H.	D	24-25	5
Witheridge, T.	M	31-33	1
Woan, D.	F	51-53	25
Wood, A.	G	21-31	374
Wood, B.	D	66-68	58
Wood, J.	F	49-50	9
Wood, R.	F	22-23	1
Woodward, K.	F	66-67	1
Woolton, T.	F	05-06	7
Woosnam, P.	F	54-58	108
Worrell, C.	D	64-66	51
Wright, G.	D	58-62	85
Wright, W.	D	58-62	1
Yardley, J.	F	24-27	31
Yews, T.	M	33-34	3

The following two players made an appearance in an FA Cup-tie and a League Cup-tie but did not play in a League match:

Bow, J.	F	34-35	1	(FA Cup)
Wedge, R.	F	62-63	1	(League Cup)

The following two were non-playing substitutes in a League game:

Wigg, R.	F	64-67
Whittington, E.	D	70 only

The Tom Johnston Goalscoring Record

Tom Johnston holds Orient's seasonal and aggregate goalscoring records. Here is a goal-by-goal breakdown. FA Cup goals shown thus (FA).

55/6
1 v Swindon T.	A	His O's debut
3 v Aldershot	H	
1 v C. Palace	A	
2 v Shrewsbury T.	H	
1 v Millwall	H	

56/7
1 v Bury	H
1 v Notts Co.	A
1 v Stoke C.	A
1 v Blackburn R.	A
1 v Swansea T.	H
1 v Sheffield Utd.	A
2 v Barnsley	H
1 v Port Vale	A
1 v Rotherham	H
1 v Bristol C.	H
1 v Fulham	A
2 v Nottm. Forest	A
1 v Huddersfield T.	H
2 v Bury	A
1 v Grimsby T.	H
2 v Stoke C.	H
1 v Middlesborough	A
1 v Doncaster R.	A
1 v West Ham	A
1 v Port Vale	H
1 v Leicester C.	H
1 v Leicester C.	A
1 v Notts Co.	H

57/8
2 v Grimsby T.	A
2 v Doncaster R.	H
1 v Bristol C.	A
2 v Charlton	A
2 v Cardiff C.	H
2 v Charlton	H
1 v West Ham	A
2 v Barnsley	H
2 v Swansea T.	H
2 v Notts Co.	H
1 v Ipswich T.	A
2 v Blackburn R.	H
1 v Sheffield Utd	A
3 v Grimsby T.	H
4 v Rotherham	H
1 v Rotherham	A
1 v Stoke C.	A
1 v Reading	H(FA)
3 v Bristol C.	H

58/9
2 v Sheffield Utd	A
1 v Brighton & H. A.	H
1 v Sunderland	H
1 v Bristol C.	A
1 v Grimsby T.	A
2 v Cardiff C.	H
2 v Barnsley	A

59/60
1 v Bristol R.	A
1 v Stoke C.	H
2 v Ipswich T.	H
1 v Stoke C.	A
1 v Brighton & H. A.	H
2 v Rotherham	H
1 v Brighton & H. A.	A
1 v Cardiff C.	A
1 v Hull C	H
1 v Sheffield Utd	A
1 v Middlesborough	H
2 v Liverpool	A
1 v Bristol C.	A
1 v Huddersfield T.	H
1 v Lincoln C.	A
1 v Sunderland	A
2 v Cardiff C.	H
1 v Hull C.	A
1 v Liverpool	H
1 v Middlesborough	A

60/1
1 v Ipswich T.	H
1 v Brighton & H. A.	A
2 v Scunthorpe Utd	A
1 v Leeds Utd	A
2 v Derby Co.	H
1 v Stoke C.	A
1 v Swansea T.	H

1 v Portsmouth	A
1 v Norwich C.	A
1 v Ipswich T.	A
1 v Scunthorpe Utd	H
1 v Portsmouth	H
1 v Stoke C.	H
1 v Norwich C.	H
1 v Gillingham	A (FA)

The above FA Cup goal is not in the order

Goals scored by Tom Johnston for Orient in other competitions

Reserves
60/1

1 v Leicester C.	A
1 v Chelsea	A

London Challenge Cup
60/1

1 v Walthamstow	H

Friendlies
56/7

2 v Charlton	H
1 v Bromley	A

57/8

2 v East Fife	H

60/1

1 v Hapoel Petach Tikva (Israel)	H

Other goals
Orient tour in Malta 56
2 v Malta Under 21s
1 v Sliema Wanderers
1 v Floriana
In Channel Islands 61
3 v Guernsey Amalgamated
Goals in Public Trials
57/8
1 for Blues v Reds
59/60
1 for Blues v Reds
60/1
1 for Reds v Blues (match one)
1 for Blues v Reds (match two)
He also scored 2 goals in the Southern
Floodlight Cup for O's in 59/60.

League and FA Cup goals scored against Orient

53/4

2 for Norwich v Orient	A

54/5

1 for Newport v Orient	H
1 for Newport v Orient	A

55/6

3 for Newport v Orient	A
1 for Newport v Orient	H

58/9

1 for Blackburn v Orient	A (FA)

Johnston's Record at a glance

Season	Club	Div.	Goals Scored	Season's Total
49/50	Kilmarnock	Scot. div 2	15	15
50/1	Kilmarnock	Scot. div 2	5	5
51/2	Oldham	3 north	3	
51/2	Darlington	3 north	9	12
52/3	Norwich C.	3 south	15	15
53/4	Norwich C.	3 south	16	16
54/5	Norwich C.	3 south	2	
54/5	Newport Co.	3 south	26	28
55/6	Newport Co.	3 south	21	
55/6	Orient	3 south	8	29
56/7	Orient	2	27	27
57/8	Orient	2	36	
57/8	Blackburn R.	2	8	44
58/9	Blackburn R.	1	15	
58/9	Orient	2	10	25
59/60	Orient	2	25	25
60/1	Orient	2	17	17
61/2	Gillingham	4	10	10

(The above includes FA Cup goals)
Johnston scored a few goals for Folkes-
stone in the Southern League in 62/3.
The Southern Floodlight Cup is now
a defunct competition. It was in operation for about 7 years.

Players who have made 200 Orient League appearances or more

A. Wood	374
S. Charlton	367
P. Allen	339(4)
F. Parker	336
S. Aldous	302
K. Facey	301
S. Bishop	296
J. Galbraith	280
R. Goddard	278
P. Welton	263
J. Townrow	254
T. Dixon	232
M. Bullock	223(8)
M. Jones	223(5)
L. Blizzard	221
P. White	221
J. Johnston	219
C. Lea	205
G. Scott	205
W. Broadbent	200

Players who have scored an aggregate of 30 or more League goals for Orient

(League appearances are shown to give
an idea of goals per game average)

Player	League Appearances	League Goals
T. Johnston	181	121
K. Facey	301	74
E. Crawford	199	68
R. McFadden	137	65
R. Tricker	130	64
M. Bullock	223(8)	61
W. Rees	184	59
D. Dunmore	147	54
D. Pacey	119	46
F. Neary	78	45
B. Fairbrother	148(14)	40
R. Heckman	87	38
R. Dalrymple	139	37
F. Beven	128	36

J. Hartburn	112	36
W. Pullen	116	35
L. Julians	67	35
F. Parker	336	35
G. Scott	205	34
D. Halliday	52	33
J. Tonner	140	33
O. Williams	162	33
C. Fletcher	120	32
H. Smith	148	31

Present Squad Aggregate goals

	League	FA Cup	League Cup	Total
P. Allen	26	1	0	27
P. Bennett	1	0	0	1
T. Brisley	8	0	0	8
M. Bullock	61	1	3	65
D. Downing	9	0	2	11
B. Fairbrother	40	6	2	48
P. Harris	4	0	0	4
R. Heppolette	6	0	0	6
P. Hoadley	4	1	0	5
G. Queen	22	0	1	23
W. Roffey	1	0	0	1
T. Walley	3	0	0	3

Please note that the above records only concern goals for Orient. Several of these players have scored League goals etc., for other clubs. Linton, Boyle, Fisher, Payne, have not scored, plus, of course, Goddard, Jackson, O'Shaughnessy.

Players Appearances and Goals scored
League, FA Cup, League Cup

	posit'n	signed	league	FA Cup	FL Cup
P. Allen	M	65	339(4)	19	16
P. Bennett	M	70	92	7	2
J. Boyle	M	73	13	4	0
T. Brisley	M	66	119(9)	7(1)	7
M. Bullock	F	68	223(8)	15	11
D. Downing	D	72	73(2)	2(2)	6
B. Fairbrother	F	67	148(14)	13	5(1)
R. Fisher	D	71	4(4)	0	2
R. Goddard	G	67	278	20	13
P. Harris	D	69	82	7	5(2)
R. Heppolette	M	72	49	5	1
P. Hoadley	D	71	116	9	6
J. Jackson	G	73	16	1	2
M. Linton	D	72	13(5)	3	0(1)
M. O'Shaughnessy	G	70	1	0	0
D. Payne	D	73	34(1)	4	4
G. Queen	F	72	67(2)	4	3
W. Roffey	D	73	20(1)	0	1
J. Walley	D	71	72(2)	8	4

The following are young Professionals with no League experience

W. Bragg	F	72
R. Broomfield	M	73
L. Cunningham	F	72

I. Filby	F	70
S. Drummy	F	72
N. Gray	Central D	73
A. Grealish	M	72
G. Hibbs	M	72
D. Mooney	F	72
G. Roeder	M	72
J. Smeulders	G	72
I. Woodward	D	71

Orient Directors through the years

P. H. Arber
W. Baxter
C. Bent-Marshall
G. Botten
H. F. Boyden
P. Boyden
R. Briggs
A. J. Byrne
W. Cornish
G. Cowan
B. Delfont
R. R. Elliott
B. Emmanuel
H. Garland-Wells
L. Grade
H. Grey Robbins
E. Girt
S. Goodger
G. H. Harris
F. F. Harris
E. Hayes
R. Holmes

G. S. Kenure
H. Lea
J. Loe
T. S. Ludford
J. McCarthy
D. McLardy
W. Moore
G. Mordall
N. Ovenden
D. J. Osborne
A. E. Page
M. E. Page
H. F. Robertson
R. L. Sharplin
P. G. Showell
F. Snewin
M. Swears
A. Unwin
G. Wells-Holland
T. Wiggins
T. Wimms
B. B. Winston
J. Woods
F. Young
H. S. Zussman

Orient Secretaries

P. Barnes	73-
C. W. H. Dean	09-30
J. Falltrick	70-3
R. Gilson	72-3 (asst. secretary)
T. W. Halsey	34-9
S. E. Hawkins	31-4 (asst. secretary)
G. A. Hicks	57-70
A. H. Huggett	53-7
R. R. Jack	46-7
F. Keatch	48-52 (asst. secretary)
J. J. Lennon	52-3
J. Phillips	30-3
T. Woodcock	00-06

Orient Managers

J. Bloomfield	68-71
J. Carey	61-3
B. Fenton	63-4
L. Gore	56, 57-8, 59-61, 63, 64-5, 65-6
R. Graham	66-8
A. Grimsdell	29-30
W. Hall	45
T. Halsey	39-40
C. Hewitt	46-8
W. Holmes	07-22
N. McBain	48-9
S. Ormerod	05-7
D. Pratt	33-5
P. Proudfoot	23-8, 31, 35-9
G. Petchey	71
J. Seed	31-3
D. Sexton	65

A. Stock	49-56, 56-7, 58-9
W. Wright	40-5, 45-6

Temporary Managers

W. Allison	31
P. Angell	68
S. White	35

Orient Trainers

P. Angell	(trainer)	67
E. Baily	(coach)	60-3
F. Bevan	(coach)	20-3
D. Clark	(coach)	66
N. Collins	(asst. trainer)	54-61
C. Durning	(asst. trainer)	12-20
G. Glidden	(trainer)	50-1
L. Gore	(trainer)	51-66
W. Hind	(asst. trainer)	20-6
A. Hird	(asst. trainer)	59-61
T. Husbands	(asst. trainer)	31-3
J. Lawrence	(asst. trainer)	20-1
T. Long	(coach)	73-
J. Mallett	(coach)	56-8
J. Martin	(trainer)	67
J. Galbraith	(coach)	38-9
A. Parsons	(trainer)	22-3
F. Powell	(trainer)	19-29
J. Pugsley	(asst. trainer)	38-40
E. Rich	(asst. trainer)	48-9
J. Richardson	(trainer)	47-54
W. Rickett	(trainer)	66-7
J. Smith	(coach)	36-7
S. White	(trainer)	33-7
W. J. Wright	(trainer)	47
W. P. Wright	(trainer)	35-40

Orient players who gained full International Caps

For Wales: T. J. Evans, 1928, E. Lawrence, 30, M. Lucas, 62, T. Mills, 34, E. Morley, 29, P. Woosnam, 58. For England: J. Townrow, 25 & 26, O. Williams, 23.

Seasonal individual goalscoring record (League)

35 by T. Johnston in 57/8.

Highest individual aggregate of League goals

121 by T. Johnston, 56-8, 59-61

Highest score by the Club in major matches

9-2 v Aldershot on 10 February 1934 in League division 3 (south). Team: Robertson; Keen, Crompton; Fogg, Fellowes, Ware; Mayson, Crawford, Halliday, Mills, Rigby. (Goals: Halliday 3, Ware 2, Mayson, Mills, Rigby, Crawford).

9-2 v Chester on 15 October 1962 in League Cup Round 3. Team: Robert-son; Charlton, Taylor; Gibbs, Bishop, Lea; Deeley, Waites, Dunmore, Graham, Wedge. (Goals: Graham 3, Waites 3, Dunmore 2, Deeley).

Obviously the goalkeepers in the above two matches are different players. Alf (ex-Bradford P.A. and Newcastle Utd) appeared in the first match and Bill (ex-Chelsea) played in the League Cuptie

Biggest margin victory

8-0 v Crystal Palace on 12 November 1955 in division 3 (south). Team: Welton; Lee, Earl; Blizzard, Aldous, McKnight; White, Facey, Burgess, Heckman, Hartburn. (Goals: Facey 3, Hartburn 2, Burgess 2, White)

Best away victory

7-1 at Exeter City on 6 November 1954 in division 3 (south). Team: Welton; Lee, Charlton; Blizzard, Aldous, McKnight; Groves, Facey, Rees, Morgan, Poulton. (Goals: Groves 3, Rees 2, Morgan, Charlton).

Heaviest defeat

0-8 home to Aston Villa on 30 January 1929 in FA Cup fourth round replay. Team: Wood; Morley, Gay; Galbraith, Eastman, Duffy; Collins, Whipp, Turnbull, Dennison, Corkindale.

Best Double

7-1 at Exeter City and 5-0 at home, 54/5.

Hat-trick in first team debut

D. Pacey v Gorleston on 3 December 1951 (at Highbury) in FA Cup first round, second replay.

Quickest hat-trick

J. Hartburn in 3.5 minutes v Shrewsbury T. on 22 January 1955 (Orient won 5-0) in division 3 (south).

Orient's Grounds

The Orient Club have played at: Millfields Road, 1881-1930; Lea Bridge, 1930-37; at Brisbane Road since 1937. They also played two home League matches (in November and December 1930) at Wembley Stadium while their Lea Bridge ground was undergoing alterations.

The first time Orient conceded more than 6 goals in a League match was on 16 April 1949 when they lost 7-1 at Torquay. It was O's 1338th League match.

The first time Orient scored more than 6 goals in a League match was when they beat Swindon Town 7-1 on 21 January 1933. It was O's 951st League match.

Up to 1947 Orient had never been beaten by more than a six goal margin in a League match. The highest number of goals conceded by them in League matches is 7 on five occasions, and in these five matches O's scored one goal in three of them and 2 goals in the other two games.

In all Orient's long history only once have they scored more League goals away than they have at home. That was in the promotion season of 61/2 when they scored 34 at home and 35 away.

Early in the 62/3 season Orient beat Manchester United 1-0 on Saturday 8 September, then beat Everton on Wednesday 12 September by 3-0. Everton went on to become League champions that season while Manchester Utd won the FA Cup.

During the 54/5 season Orient played three League games in four days over Easter and lost all three. Yet the length of time between their previous three defeats was from 23 October to 17 March and in that same season they went from 23 October to 8 April without an away defeat.

Orient have played Bristol City more times than they've played any other club in League matches.

Denis Pacey scored more FA Cup goals for Orient than any other player. He scored 12 in all: 6 in 51/2, 1 in 52/3, 5 in 53/4.

In a spell of six consecutive matches during the 55/6 season Orient scored 31 goals in this order 8-7, 4-4, 4-4, four of the matches were League fixtures, the other two were FA Cup games.

When Orient beat Bury 2-0 on 28 April 1962 and so clinched promotion in division 1 it was their first home League victory for 3 months. Their previous home win being 3-0 against

Walsall on 13 January 1962.

In the 54/5 season they beat Shrewsbury Town 5-0 and in that match scored 3 goals in a 3.5 minute period. The following season they defeated Shrewsbury Town 5-2 and 3 of the goals were scored in a period of 4 minutes, (both matches were League fixtures).

Orient won on each of their first four away League match visits to Sheffield Utd yet did not beat the Sheffield Club at home until their seventeenth attempt.

The first club to visit Wales for a League match was Orient when, on 30 August 1920, they drew 0-0 at Cardiff City; Cardiff presented O's with an illuminated address (plaque) as a memento.

When Orient were already doomed to relegation to division three toward the end of the 65/6 season, their last three home matches were against the three teams involved in the promotion race at the top: Southampton, Man-

chester City and Coventry City, but O's avoided defeat in all three games (all were drawn).

To avoid relegation at the end of the 26/7 season Orient had to win their last League match at Reading, and fellow strugglers Darlington had to drop a point versus Chelsea. O's won 1-0 at Reading thanks to a Jack Gardner penalty kick and Darlington did drop a point when Chelsea equalised just 40 seconds from the end of the match! and so it was Darlington and not Orient who were relegated.

The honour for the quickest goal scored by Orient in an FA Cup-tie goes to Norman Deeley, who netted after only 1.5 minutes of the round four tie v West Ham at Brisbane Road in the 63/4 season. When O's returned to the 2nd division after 27 years in 56/7 they had five players who were thirty or over for the first match v Nottingham Forest.

G. Sutherland scored 3 goals for Orient v Ipswich T. (at Ipswich) in a 4-4 draw on 17 September 1949. In the return match at Leyton, Orient won 4-4, Sutherland again scoring three times—the only time that an Orient player has achieved this against the same club in one season.

Joe Elwood was the club's first ever substitute to replace a player on the field of play, v Preston North End (at Leyton) on 4 September 1965 when he replaced the injured J. McGeorge under the new rule.

The two youngest Orient players to appear in the club's League eleven are Paul Went and Tommy Taylor. Both were under 16 years of age.

Two of the smallest players ever to appear in the Football League were with Orient: F. Lemay (32/3) and I. Miles (34/7).

The record number of consecutive League appearances is held by A. Wood. That was 228, 21/6.

Arthur Woods holds the record number of League appearances for Orient: 374 between 1921 and 1931. (Peter Allen is catching up, with 339 (4) at the close of 73/4.)

Quite a number of players have scored a goal for Orient in under a minute but the two quickest traced are J. Andrews v Sheffield Utd (at Leyton)

The well known voicè! Keith Simpson, the man behind the Brisbane Rd microphone

in 58/9, and P. Allen at Millwall in 70/1. Andrews' goal came in 30 seconds, Allen's in 32 seconds.

Brothers with the Orient at the same time have included:

George and Jim Lamberton (05/6)

T. and J. Caldwell (07/8)

Sam, Jack, and J. T. Tonner in the early 20s.

Bob and Jack Duffus (22/3)

Tom and Owen Williams (21/3)

Malcolm and Ian Filby (for Juniors and Reserves, 68/72).

Bobby and Les Moss (for O's Minor Teams, 69/72). Bobby appeared in the League side also.

Alan and Len Cheesewright appeared in O's colts teams in the early 1960s.

J. and T. Gordon both had trials for the Club during the 32/3 season.

Ron and Ken Crayden played for the colts (57/9).

Ron Willis was first team goalkeeper, 65/7; his brother Alan played for colts 67/8.

W. Hales played in Orient's League team in 10/11. His son Billy played for O's League team, 30/3.

Len Julians holds Orient's reserve goal-scoring record with 45 in 56/7.

Orient have only completed a season without losing at home in League matches on one occasion; that was 13/4 when they won all bar 5 home matches, and they were drawn.

Orient have never conceded more than seven goals in a League match. They have conceded 7 goals on five occasions, losing 7-1 three times and 7-2 twice.

There were ten seasons from 1905, when Orient came into League football, to 1915, when war halted the League competition. Only one player appeared in at least one League match in all those seasons, that was goalkeeper Billy Bower.

Bert Kingaby scored O's first ever goal in League football on 2 September 1905 at Leicester Fosse. Fred Tully scored O's first goal at Brisbane Road v Cardiff City on 28 August 1937. Dave Sexton scored Orient's first goal in div. 2 after a 27 year gap, on 18 August 1956 v Nott'm Forest, and Derek Gibbs scored the first ever goal in div. 1 on 18 August 1962 v Arsenal.

Orient's only appearance in the final of London's five-a-side championships was 6 May 1958. The team of Groombridge, Lea, Woosnam, Andrews, and Julians reached the finals by beating Millwall 1-0, Spurs 3-1, QPR 1-0, and in the final they beat Crystal Palace 1-0.

The best FA Cup runs were reaching round six in 25/6, 53/4 and 71/2.

55/6 was Orient's best scoring season at home, with 76 goals. It was also the best in a number of other aspects: most wins, 29; most points, 66; most League goals, 106.

61/2 had the best away record: played 21, won 11, drawn 5, lost 5. And by conceding only 40 goals in

61/2, they had the best average in the Football League for that season.

Orient attendances

Maximum attendances at Orient's three grounds:

Millfields Road: 63000 v Newcastle Utd (FA Cup, 26)

Lea Bridge Road: 20400 v Millwall (Div. 3 (south) 37)

Brisbane Road: 34345 v West Ham (FA Cup 64); 33383 v Birmingham City (Div. 2, 72)

Three of the quickest hat-tricks ever scored in the League involved Orient. W. Lane scored 3 goals in 3 minutes for Watford v Clapton Orient on 20 December 1933. J. Scarth scored 3 in 2.5 minutes for Gillingham v Leyton Orient on 1 November 1952. J. Hartburn (as mentioned earlier) W. Lane later played for Orient in 37/8 season.

Orient Club Colours

Red shirts (white O on back), white shorts   1881-1899

Blue shirts (white O on back), white shorts   1899-1905

Red, white and green striped shirts, white shorts   1905-1909

White shirts with red V, black shorts   1909-1932

Red and white hooped shirts, black shorts with red and white seam   1932-1943

White shirts with blue V, black shorts   1944-1947

Blue shirts, white shorts   1947-1965

Blue shirts with thick white sash, white shorts   July-December 1965

Blue shirts, white shorts   1965-1966

Blue shirts, blue shorts   1966-1967

Red shirts, red shorts   1967-1973

Red shirts with white collars, white shorts   1973-

116